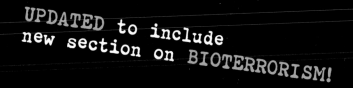

UPDATED to include
new section on BIOTERRORISM!

R E A K

disease
detectives
at work

Mark P. Friedlander Jr.

Lerner Publications Company ■ Minneapolis

Dedicated to Dorothy

Special thanks to Leonard T. Kurland, M.D., Ph.D., Professor Emeritus of Epidemiology, Mayo Clinic, for his helpful direction; to Jennifer L. Sturges, Chief of Information Systems, The Krasnow Institute for Advanced Study, George Mason University, for her research guidance; to Robert O. Brennan, M.D., F.A.C.P., Medical Associates of Central Virginia, for his medical observations; and to Amanda S. Birnbaum, M.P.H., Department of Epidemiology, University of Minnesota, for her help in preparing and fact-checking this book.

Page two: A researcher in protective clothing removes human immuno-deficiency virus (HIV) from a culture for testing.

Lerner Publications Company
A Division of Lerner Publishing Group
241 First Avenue North
Minneapolis, Minnesota 55401 U.S.A.

Website address: www.lernerbooks.com

Library of Congress Cataloging-in-Publication Data

Friedlander, Mark P.
    Outbreak : disease detectives at work / by Mark P. Friedlander Jr.—Updated ed.
       p.   cm.
    Summary: Describes the field of epidemiology and its history, presenting historical and modern case studies and biological explanations of some diseases and a discussion of the microbes most likely to be used by bioterrorists.
    Includes index.
    ISBN: 0-8225-0948-2 (lib. bdg. : alk. paper)
    1. Epidemiology—Juvenile literature. [1. Epidemiology. 2. Diseases.]
    I. Title.
RA653.5 .F75 2003
614.4—dc21   2002006836

Manufactured in the United States of America
1 2 3 4 5 6 – JR – 08 07 06 05 04 03

CONTENTS

FOREWORD

This book provides a history of epidemic infectious diseases, such as the plague, smallpox, influenza, Ebola, and AIDS. It introduces the student to epidemiology—the study of disease occurrence in populations. Epidemiology is not the same as medical care of patients. The epidemiologist, or disease detective, looks at medical care in an entire community or country as a source of epidemiologic data. These data may include the description of a disease—how old are the people who are affected? Do more men or more women get the disease? What are their jobs? The data may also show the geographic and seasonal distribution of cases—whether the disease happens in just one city, state, or region, for example—or whether it strikes only in summer.

The essence of epidemiology involves understanding a disease and its causes. This involves three main steps. First, a physician describes and records what he or she has observed, including the symptoms of a disease. Second, laboratory tests help develop a specific diagnosis, such as "German measles." Finally, the epidemiologist compares the characteristics of people who are affected by the disease with those of people who are not affected.

The science of epidemiology began with the battle against infectious diseases such as smallpox and influenza. Early in the twentieth century, epidemiologists successfully extended their methods to include conditions such as mercury poisoning, vitamin deficiencies, and hormonal abnormalities such as diabetes and goiter. In recent decades, epidemiologists have studied diseases such as cancer, heart disease, and stroke. The result is a better understanding of how these disorders work and a clearer path to identifying their causes and treatments.

This book is a tribute to many of the clinical investigators and epidemiologists who have conducted studies at universities and at centers such as the Pasteur Institute in Paris, France, the National Institutes of Health in Bethesda, Maryland, and the Centers for Disease Control and Prevention in Atlanta, Georgia. Students will learn about critical public health questions and their solutions through epidemiology. Some who read this book will become the scientists who identify and control risk factors for diseases of the future.

Leonard T. Kurland, M.D., Ph.D.
Professor Emeritus of Epidemiology
Mayo Clinic
Rochester, Minnesota

THE BLUE MEN

On the morning of September 25, 1944, a ragged old man was carried by ambulance to the Beekman–Downtown Hospital in New York City. He was a homeless man who had passed out in the street and was in a state of shock. Most remarkably, the man's nose, lips, ears, and fingers were sky blue—a beautiful but unhealthy color.

After being treated in the hospital, the man began to recover. The blue turned back to a healthier pink. The doctors suspected gas poisoning—but where and how? Before the day was over, 10 more older homeless men were brought to the hospital—and all were bright blue.

The hospital called in the chief epidemiologist, or medical detective, of the New York City Department of Health, Dr. Morris Greenberg, and another department epidemiologist, Dr. Ottavio Pelliteri. One of the blue men died that night, but the others seemed to be recovering. The doctors at the hospital and the epidemiologists began to realize that these cases were not gas poisoning. As the men became well enough to answer questions, it became clear that the only thing they all had in common was that they had eaten breakfast at a local cafeteria, the Eclipse, a place where homeless and poor people could get cheap meals. Each man had eaten oatmeal, rolls, and coffee and had fallen sick within half an hour of the meal.

In New York City in 1944, a number of men fell ill with a mysterious ailment that turned their skin bright blue.

The doctors suspected food poisoning, but the onset of illness had been sudden for each victim. This was not typical of food poisoning. Could it be drugs? Blood tests showed that none of the men had used drugs.

When the doctors went to the restaurant to investigate, they found filth—roaches, flies, old grease covering the kitchen walls and ceiling, garbage on the floor mixed with dirt, leaking sewer pipes—but none of these had directly caused the illness. In addition, the cooks reported that they had fed over one hundred customers at breakfast that day, and no one else became ill.

Dr. Greenberg and Dr. Pelliteri gathered samples of everything that was used to prepare the meals the 11 homeless men had eaten: ground coffee, sugar, evaporated milk, rolls, dry oatmeal, and salt. The cook explained that he had used five pounds of dry oatmeal mixed with four gallons of water and a handful of salt to make oatmeal for the customers. He showed the scientists the can of salt he had used. Next to that can was another can that looked just like it.

When Dr. Greenberg looked into the second can, he realized that although it looked like salt, it wasn't. Instead, it was saltpeter, or sodium nitrate, normally used to make corned beef and pastrami. Still, this could not have poisoned the men.

Dr. Greenberg and Dr. Pelliteri took the samples back to the Health Department laboratory. To their surprise, they learned that the can that they thought contained sodium *nitrate* actually contained sodium *nitrite*. Both substances look and taste the same, just like table salt; but sodium nitrite is a mild poison.

The homeless men's symptoms fit the picture of sodium nitrite poisoning. But there was still another puzzle. If sodium nitrite had been in the oatmeal instead of salt, and over 100 people had eaten the oatmeal, why had only 11 men become sick?

Then Dr. Greenberg remembered something from his youth. While most people put sugar on their oatmeal, some older people liked to sprinkle salt on theirs. He and Dr. Pelliteri went back to the cafeteria to check out the saltshakers. There were 17 shakers, one at each table. Sixteen shakers contained salt. One contained sodium nitrite.

Although the 11 men had not eaten at the same time, they had all eaten at the same table. They had all sprinkled extra "salt" on their oatmeal—just enough sodium nitrite to give them the blues.

Chapter One

EPIDEMIOLOGY:
THE STUDY OF DISEASE

- *Over half the passengers on a cruise ship in the Caribbean Sea come down with severe diarrhea.*
- *An eruption of tuberculosis sweeps through a Los Angeles high school, infecting one-third of its students.*
- *Thousands of people in Milwaukee suddenly become ill from drinking tap water.*

These outbreaks of illness, like the cases of sodium nitrite poisoning among homeless men in New York, were epidemics. An epidemic is an unusually high number of cases of a disease among a group of people. An epidemic disease that spreads throughout an entire country or continent, or the whole world, is called a pandemic. (Sometimes, however, even a massive pandemic is referred to as an epidemic.) AIDS is a pandemic. Some epidemics or pandemics develop slowly, and other outbreaks are sudden and unexpected.

Epidemiology is the study of the distribution, identification, and nature of health and disease. While physicians treat and study health and disease in individuals, epidemiologists look at health and disease in a population. Epidemiologists' areas of study include chronic diseases such as cancer and heart disease; infectious diseases such as the flu or measles; reproductive, maternal, and child health; nutrition and health; violence; injury

A masked researcher examines lines of bacteria growing in culture.

prevention; genetics; aging; and disabilities.

Infectious disease epidemiology, a major focus of this book, is a core field within epidemiology. Infectious disease epidemiologists focus on the incidence, distribution, and control of infectious diseases—those that can spread. These epidemiologists hunt for the causes of diseases that affect populations and try to stop the spread of those diseases. Infectious disease epidemiologists are disease detectives.

Many diseases that produce epidemics are caused by microbes—microscopic organisms—that cause contagious, or infectious, diseases. Microbes include bacteria, viruses, parasites, and fungi. Microbes spread disease by traveling through the air and in water, bodily fluids, and food. Diseases may spread from animals or insects to humans, or from person to person through contact with bodily fluids (for example, droplets produced by coughing and sneezing). Thus, the disease detective must search not only for the cause of an epidemic disease, but also for the means of transmission—how it spreads.

You have probably read about the devastating epidemics of the past, such as the plague, which destroyed one-third of the population of Europe during the Middle Ages. But epidemics are not just something from days gone by—they still affect people all around the world. Some epidemics, such as AIDS, are massive. Thanks to the work of epidemiologists, many modern epidemics have been contained, or stopped. The work of these men and women is often slow and difficult, and sometimes dangerous.

THE BEGINNING OF EPIDEMIOLOGY

In 1830, a rumor swept through London, England, that a deadly and unknown disease was spreading from India to England. At the time, England controlled India as part of its widespread British Empire. Most people in London paid little attention to this rumor.

Many poor citizens in London lived in filth and squalor. The streets were dirt and mud. Garbage and human and animal waste ended up in the Thames River, the source of most Londoners' water supply. Other waste seeped into the common public wells around the city. People drank, cooked, and washed with the same water into which waste was dumped. As the population grew, the water became even more polluted, but most people did not worry about how crowded and dirty the bulging city had become. By 1832, the new disease, cholera, was not just a rumor in London but a terrible reality—an epidemic.

Cholera is caused by a bacterium, *Vibrio cholerae,* that can survive for long periods of time in water. When a person swallows water containing cholera bacteria, acid in the stomach may kill the bacteria. But if the bacteria survive the stomach acid, they move to the intestines, where they multiply rapidly. The person may develop sudden and violent diarrhea, vomiting, and fever, followed by death. A cholera victim's dehydrated body shrinks into a shriveled skeleton, and the skin turns black and blue. Death from cholera is often dramatic and swift.

Thousands of different types of bacteria exist all around us. Bacteria are single-celled organisms that are usually encased in a rigid cell wall. Some can move using hairlike cilia or long, tail-like flagella that stick out from their bodies. Most bacteria are harmless—and many are beneficial, such as those that live in our intestines and help us digest food. But bacteria that produce disease, such as *Vibrio cholerae,* can be very dangerous. They release toxins (poisons) that cause damage to their host. A host may be a plant, insect, animal, or human.

In the early nineteenth century, no one knew that diseases were caused by microorganisms, or germs, such as bacteria and viruses. These tiny organisms are invisible to the naked eye. It wasn't until the late 1800s that scientists began to understand that germs cause disease. But even in the early 1800s, there were a few doctors who believed that dirt and filth bred disease, although they did not know why.

An English doctor named John Snow was one of those. He guessed that dirty water held the key to the spread of cholera. In 1848, Dr. Snow began collecting records of cholera deaths, noting where the most deaths occurred and who supplied water to those neighborhoods. At the time, eight water companies provided water to different parts of London. Dr. Snow noticed that cholera rates were highest in areas where the water was supplied by two companies, the Lambeth Company and the Southwark and Vauxhall Company. These companies both drew their water supply from the sewage-filled Thames River.

When a wave of cholera cases swept through the Golden Square neighborhood of London in 1854, Dr. Snow began to keep more detailed records of deaths. He became more and more convinced that the cause of cholera was in the water.

Next, he went from house to house in a neighborhood called Soho, where many people were dying of cholera. He asked many questions. He learned that the people who had died had drawn their water from a public pump at the corner of Broad and Cambridge Streets. He guessed that the water at the Broad Street pump was causing the disease. But he also found out that 10 people who lived closer to other public pumps had also gotten cholera. This fact cast doubt on his theory.

Dr. Snow visited the families of those 10 victims to get more information. From them he learned that 5 of the 10 had been

Many poor Londoners in the 1800s lived in filth and squalor. The field of epidemiology began when Dr. John Snow investigated the source of a cholera outbreak in the city in 1854.

going to the Broad Street pump because they thought the water tasted better, and 3 of the victims were children who attended a school near that pump.

On September 7, 1854, Dr. Snow met with city leaders. He revealed his findings and requested that the Broad Street pump be closed. Some officials laughed at his theory. What good would it do to shut down a water pump? But since no one else had a solution or a cure for the deadly epidemic, the city officials agreed to remove the pump handle. The epidemic subsided in that area of the city.

Following his success with the Broad Street pump, Dr. Snow broadened his study of cholera deaths. He determined that there were nine times as many deaths in areas where water was supplied by the Southwark and Vauxhall Company as there were in areas supplied by the Lambeth Company. While Southwark and Vauxhall drew water from a very polluted part of the Thames River, the Lambeth Company had switched its water source to a less polluted section of the river. From this data, Snow concluded that cholera was caused by polluted water. He had begun the art and science of studying epidemics and is considered the "father" of epidemiology.

MODERN EPIDEMIOLOGY

The modern science of epidemiology involves much more than studying sudden outbreaks of disease. Microbes are not the only cause of disease within a population. Too much cholesterol in the diet can lead to heart disease. Cigarette smoking within a population can result in an increase in the number of cases of lung cancer.

The evidence that supports the connection between a cause, such as smoking, and a disease, like lung cancer, is referred to as a statistical association. Not all smokers develop lung cancer, and nonsmokers also suffer from lung cancer. But statistics show that more smokers than nonsmokers develop lung cancer. This relationship, or association, is important. For an epidemiologist to make a valid statistical association of a disease and a cause, he or she must analyze the makeup of the group that is

affected. Who is getting the disease? Is there really an association between the assumed cause and the disease itself, or is the
observed association a matter of chance?

Suppose, for example, that the number of cases of AIDS in
the United States increased by 6 percent over a given time, and
during that same period, the value of the stock market also
went up 6 percent. Because the percentage is the same, there
would appear to be a statistical association between the increase
in AIDS and the increase in the stock market. But the growth
of the stock market wouldn't have anything to do with the
spread of AIDS—the 6 percent rise would be simply coinciden-
tal. A statistical association alone is not enough to determine
the cause of a disease—there must be some biological mechanism that could cause the disease, like the sodium nitrite that
poisoned the "blue men" in New York.

Dr. Gary Friedman, an epidemiologist and author of a text-
book on the subject, outlined another example of a false association for disease. He asked this question: Is a man or woman
who has had a parent die more likely to suffer from back pain
than a person whose parents are still alive? He found no relationship between the death of a parent and low back pain for
people aged 30 to 39. On the other hand, 84 percent of his research subjects between the ages of 50 and 59 who had at least
one parent die did suffer from low back pain. When he
grouped the statistics from all subjects from age 30 to 59, the
data appeared to show that parental loss was related to low
back pain.

But this result was nonsense. Dr. Friedman had not ac-
counted for another factor, or variable. Men and women aged
50 to 59 are more likely to have had at least one parent die
than people aged 30 to 39. Also, people in their 50s are more

likely than people in their 30s to suffer from low back pain. The pain is most likely due to the aging process—it has nothing to do with the death of a parent. Still, when the statistics concerning people in all age groups from 30 to 59 were combined, they showed that more people who had a parent die have low back pain than do those whose parents are still alive. The results were not scientifically valid, because of a false association that had been introduced by the ages of people in the study. Epidemiologists call this false association confounding. In this study, age was acting as a confounder of the association between death of a parent and back pain.

By gathering statistical data according to carefully framed rules, epidemiologists can determine the relationship between a disease and its possible cause. Epidemiologists use what is called a cohort study to establish the risk of getting a disease. A cohort is a selected population of people, such as all the residents of a community or all the customers who ate hamburgers at a certain restaurant within a given time frame.

THE ROCHESTER EPIDEMIOLOGY PROJECT

For decades, the Mayo Clinic, a large hospital in Rochester, Minnesota, has kept health records for people living in the region. These records provide precious information for epidemiologists.

In 1907, a Mayo physician, Dr. Henry Plummer, began keeping detailed medical records about people living in the city of Rochester and surrounding Olmsted County. Thirty years later, Dr. Joseph Berkson developed a more elaborate index system, using a three-digit code to keep track of the records. Then, in the 1960s, a young doctor named Leonard T. Kurland realized that these medical records represented an epidemiological gold mine. He saw that he could build a database for population-based studies of the causes and outcomes of disease.

Since the records covered a long period of time and a specific region, epidemiologists could study diseases that occurred in this population to calculate how often a certain disease could be expected to occur naturally in the population at large. This would help doctors to know if the number of cases of a particular disease was higher than average within a certain group of people. For example, by studying the Mayo Clinic data, scientists might learn that a disease such as meningitis (inflammation of the tissue that envelops the brain and spinal cord) occurs naturally at a rate of one case per year among 10,000 people in the United States. If eight or nine cases suddenly appear within a short period of time in a community, then the researchers would suspect that a specific event or mechanism might be causing the outbreak.

Dr. Kurland began his data system, called the Rochester Epidemiology Project, in 1966. At first, records were kept by hand, then on paper tape, punched cards, magnetic tape, and finally on computers. The data provide a baseline to measure the normal frequency of various diseases in a population. This statistical baseline has given public health doctors everywhere the necessary information to sound the alarm when they discover that the incidence of a disease has increased. Hundreds of studies have used this data.

CENTERS OF EPIDEMIOLOGY

Epidemiologists work for universities and public health agencies in cities, states, and countries around the world. The World Health Organization (WHO), an international public health organization affiliated with the United Nations, was established in 1946. It is headquartered in Geneva, Switzerland, and is controlled by the World Health Assembly, made up of the health ministers of 191 member countries. WHO helps track diseases, coordinates global health projects, and provides funds for health projects around the world.

In the United States, the most important public health agency is the Centers for Disease Control and Prevention (CDC) in Atlanta, Georgia. The CDC tracks emerging diseases and epidemics across the nation and alerts state health departments to potential problems. The agency identifies trends in public health and informs and educates people about health problems. It deals with a wide range of health issues in addition to infectious diseases. These include mental retardation, birth defects, school nutrition, and injury, violence, and suicide prevention. But the CDC's most dramatic work happens when scientists from the agency act as a medical "SWAT" team, rushing to the scene of a disease outbreak.

The CDC stores hundreds of thousands of specimens of viruses, bacteria, parasites, and other microbes for reference. Researchers use these samples to determine the cause of a disease by matching the characteristics and shape of the new microbe with those of the stored samples. Microbe samples are first labeled and catalogued, then frozen and stored in negative-pressure rooms. If there is a leak or break in the seals of a negative-pressure room, all air will flow from the outside to the inside, keeping the microbes contained.

When scientists want to test for the presence of a microbe, they place a drop of blood or other body fluid from the infected person in a petri dish. A petri dish is a round, shallow glass or plastic dish filled with a culture of rich nutrients such as agar (a nutrient extracted from seaweed), in which microbes will normally grow and multiply. Scientists look at samples of the new, multiplying microbes under a microscope and compare them with the samples stored at the CDC. The process is similar to that of a detective matching a suspect's fingerprints with samples kept by the FBI. Scientists can also identify a

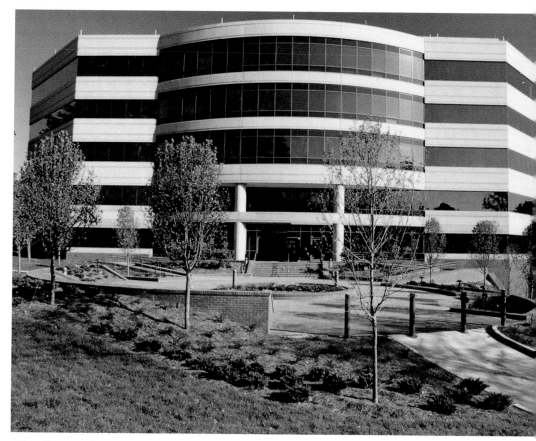

The Centers for Disease Control and Prevention, in Atlanta, Georgia, is one of the top research centers in the world.

microbe by a process known as immunocytochemistry, which involves the use of antibodies (proteins that are part of the human immune system) and color dyes.

CDC research labs are numbered as levels 1 through 4, according to their biosafety level. In a Level 1 laboratory, scientists work with ordinary organisms that do not cause disease. At Level 2, the work involves microbes that cause mild

A researcher at the CDC wears a tightly sealed blue Chemturion suit to do research in the "hot zone."

diseases, such as viruses that cause the common cold or bacteria that cause diarrhea. In a Level 3 lab, the microbes being examined may cause a serious disease, but one for which there is a vaccination or medicine available, such as rabies, Rocky Mountain spotted fever, yellow fever, Q fever, Rift Valley fever, or botulism. Doctors working in a Level 3 lab must be vaccinated for the contagious diseases with which they are working.

For the life-threatening microbes for which there is no vaccine and no cure, the work is done in a Level 4 lab—called the "hot zone." To enter the hot zone, an investigator must pass through several chambers. In the first room are lockers and a dressing area, where workers remove their clothes, shoes, rings, and other jewelry. They dress in full coveralls, taping their sleeves where they join gloves and their legs where they join socks. Next, they don a bright blue "Chemturion suit," a pressurized, helmeted, booted, gloved "space suit." When investigators leave Level 4, they must go through a decontamination shower before removing the Chemturion suit. There are only two Level 4 laboratories in the United States and just a few elsewhere in the world.

Chapter Two

A CLOSER LOOK AT MICROBES

When officers of the Epidemic Intelligence Service—the elite corps of medical detectives at the Centers for Disease Control and Prevention—head to the heart of an outbreak of any new or mysterious disease, they must try to identify the microbe, if any, that caused the disease. Diseases may be caused by many other things as well, such as genetic factors, toxic chemicals, or vitamin deficiencies. But most epidemics are the result of microbes, which are tiny organisms that can be seen only with a microscope.

Microbe and *germ* are words that generally describe microscopic invaders that cause contagious, or infectious, diseases. There are three major types of microbes: bacteria, viruses, and parasites. The most likely cause of an epidemic disease is either a bacterium or a virus. Some infectious diseases, such as malaria and sleeping sickness, are caused by single-celled parasites. Diseases such as Rocky Mountain spotted fever and typhus are caused by a group of bacteria called rickettsia. There are many microbes that spread from animals or insects to humans. Malaria is spread by the bite of a mosquito, for example, and Rocky Mountain spotted fever and Lyme disease are carried by ticks.

These red blood cells are infected with the parasite that causes malaria. Parasites are multiplying in the two cells at the right. Eventually the cells will burst, releasing parasites into the bloodstream.

BACTERIA

A bacterium is a single-celled organism. It may be shaped like a ball, rod, or coil. Hairlike flagella stick out like flowing arms from some bacteria, allowing them to move. Mostly, they travel with the flow of fluids. Like other single-celled creatures, bacteria require nutrients and oxygen, and they reproduce by dividing.

Bacteria cause damage to the human body by releasing chemical poisons. These poisons kill human cells, producing symptoms of illness.

According to Dr. Rita Colwell, a biologist at the University of Maryland who has devoted many years to studying microbes, there are anywhere from three hundred thousand to one million species of bacteria. So far, scientists have identified only two thousand of them.

Many major epidemics have been caused by bacteria. Bubonic plague, or Black Death as the plague was called, killed thousands of people in medieval Europe. It was caused by the bacterium *Yersinia pestis* and was spread by fleas that had fed on the blood of infected rats. Cholera is caused by the bacterium *Vibrio cholerae,* which lives in contaminated water or food.

Cholera epidemics still happen in places with a limited supply of clean drinking water. In the summer of 1994, thousands of refugees fleeing brutal killing in Rwanda, Africa, crowded along Rwanda's western border. They used the nearby waters for sewage disposal as well as for washing and drinking. The conditions were perfect for cholera bacteria to breed, resulting in an outbreak of the disease. In some areas of South America and India that do not have good sanitation systems and clean drinking water, many people die of cholera. In the United States, cholera outbreaks are rare, but they do occur.

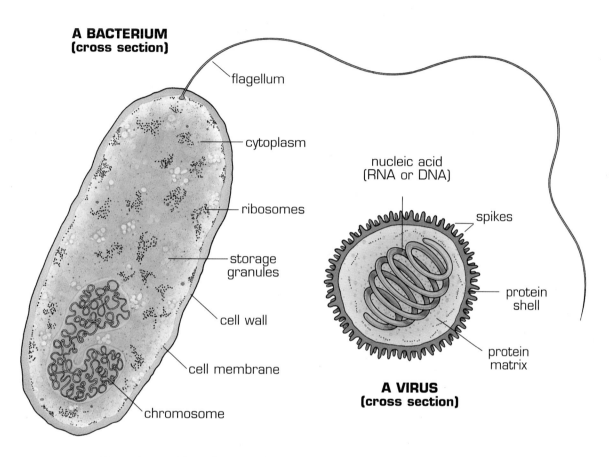

**A BACTERIUM
(cross section)**

flagellum

cytoplasm

ribosomes

storage
granules

cell wall

cell membrane

chromosome

nucleic acid
(RNA or DNA)

spikes

protein
shell

protein
matrix

**A VIRUS
(cross section)**

Bacteria are 10 to 30 times larger than the smallest virus. Even the largest virus is only about the size of the smallest bacterium.

The lung disease tuberculosis, or TB, is caused by a type of bacterium known as a mycobacterium. TB bacteria travel in water vapor particles that are released into the air when a person infected with TB coughs or sneezes. Tuberculosis is a serious problem around the world, especially among poor and homeless people. It is rarely transmitted outdoors in the open air. Most often, it spreads in confined public areas such as hospitals.

Generally, bacterial diseases can be treated by medicines called antibiotics. The most well-known antibiotic is penicillin.

VIRUSES

Bacteria are so small that they can only be seen under a microscope. But viruses are even smaller than that—they can only be seen under the most powerful microscopes, electron microscopes, which can magnify objects one hundred thousand times their actual size. If a bacterium were the size of a basketball, then a virus might be the size of a marble.

A virus is the smallest and simplest of life-forms. It is a protein shell enclosing a core of nucleic acid. (Nucleic acids such as RNA and DNA are the molecules in a cell that carry hereditary information and direct the cell's activity.) There are more than 1,400 known viruses. They have many shapes, but most are round or cylindrical.

By itself, a virus is totally passive. It cannot eat or reproduce or do anything at all until it gains entry into a host. Once inside a host, a virus locks onto the wall of a cell. The virus finds receptors on the cell surface that fit like puzzle pieces with protein molecules on the surface of the virus. Then the virus chemically drills into the cell, or, as some scientists suggest, it is "invited" in. But a virus is a terrible guest. It goes immediately to the nucleus of the cell and forces the cell to become a manufacturing plant to make more viruses. Within an hour, a cell produces one hundred new, identical viruses, which pop out of that cell to attack more and more cells. Within seven hours, a single virus can multiply to a hundred thousand viruses. Some viruses fill a cell and burst out of it, while others bud out onto the cell's surface. A viral attack can bring on disease symptoms quickly. Smallpox, yellow fever, mumps, measles, chicken pox, polio, and flu are some of the commonly known diseases caused by viruses.

THE DISCOVERY OF MICROBES

The first person to consider the idea of a microscopic living organism was the Roman writer Varro. During the first century B.C., he suggested that people became sick because they breathed in "tiny animals," or "animalcules," that were invisible to the eye. But it took more than 1,500 years before his theory caught on.

The second clue came from a Dutch cloth merchant, Antoni van Leeuwenhoek, who lived from 1632 to 1723. Leeuwenhoek devoted much of his time to his hobby of lens grinding. He hoped to improve the glasses he used to examine the texture of cloth and draperies. As his lenses became better, he began to examine water. He wanted to see if there was any difference between rainwater, well water, seawater, or water from melted snow. What he found was that water contained small, squiggly "things" that no one had seen before. He referred to them as "wee animalcules."

The origin and function of these animalcules remained a mystery until 1857, when the French chemist and medical scientist Louis Pasteur established that diseases were caused by bacteria. While working to understand why some bottles of wine were bitter, Pasteur discovered that bacteria caused wine to ferment (undergo a chemical change). He also learned that he could control bacteria with heat. The process of killing germs with heat is called *pasteurization* after Pasteur.

During this same period, a German physician, Robert Koch, developed a technique for growing colonies of bacteria. He extracted a sugar called agar from seaweed and found that it worked well as a culture medium. The ability to grow large quantities of bacteria enabled him to connect diseases to specific bacteria.

Toward the end of the nineteenth century, scientists and doctors began to accept the germ theory—the idea that infectious agents, or germs, caused diseases. Then, in 1892, a Russian

(Left) *Louis Pasteur discovered that diseases can be spread by bacteria.*

(Below) *A nineteenth-century microscope that may have been used by Pasteur*

The German physician Robert Koch was the first person to isolate the bacterium responsible for tuberculosis, a devastating disease that still affects people around the world.

scientist, Dimitrii V. Ivanovsky, made another discovery. Using a special filter called a Chamberland filter-candle, which had pores so small that bacteria could not pass through it, Ivanovsky realized that some germs *could* pass through the filter. These germs were smaller than bacteria. They could not be seen with a microscope.

Six years later, Dutch scientist Martinus W. Beijerinck confirmed this finding. But it was not until 1930, when German scientists developed the technology necessary to build an electron microscope, that people could actually see viruses.

Chapter Three

GREAT PLAGUES
OF HISTORY
BUBONIC PLAGUE, SMALLPOX, AND ANTHRAX

When epidemiologists from the CDC or the World Health Organization race to investigate some new outbreak of disease, they go armed with all the knowledge of modern science. They know to question whether the outbreak is related to a chemical poison or to a disease-causing microbe. They know they must investigate the way the disease spreads. They also know that they must try to find the source of the chemical or the breeding place of the microorganism. Finally, they know they must try to control the epidemic and prevent future outbreaks.

But the knowledge we take for granted has been long and slow in coming. Up until the late 1800s, people could only guess at what might be causing the terrible plagues that killed millions of victims. No one had any idea how these plagues spread, how to prevent them, or how to cure them.

THE BLACK DEATH

In the fall of 1347, bubonic plague arrived in Italy. Ships bringing silk, spices, and precious metals from the Orient sailed to the ports of Messina, Sicily, and Genoa in Italy. As the ships docked at the piers, crowds came to meet them, expecting to

A 1564 illustration shows Spanish priest Petrus Martinius (right) *and his monks nursing and burying plague victims.*

see wonderful new wares and hear exciting stories. Instead, what greeted them was a horror beyond their understanding.

On board the ships were dead bodies and sick and dying men. Their faces were covered with black and blue splotches; their bodies looked like skeletons. They had grotesque, bulbous growths and pus-filled sores. Although some people in Europe had heard stories about this terrible disease, no one had seen it up close.

The plague began with swelling of the lymph glands in the groin, neck, and armpits. These swellings, or *buboes* (from which the name *bubonic* comes), grew to the size of an egg. Dark splotches appeared on the skin, along with boils oozing pus.

The wisdom of the time held that diseases were caused by body fluids being out of balance. The doctors called these fluids *humors*. The term had nothing to do with a jolly mood. According to the theory of humors, the body contained four basic liquids—blood from the heart, phlegm from the brain, yellow bile from the liver, and black bile from the spleen. Doctors believed that when these humors were out of balance, sickness would result. They also believed that certain diseases were caused by poisonous gases that floated up from swamps. They called these vapors *miasmas*. People built fires or carried bouquets of flowers and sweet herbs to ward off the foul vapors.

Scientists have since discovered that bubonic plague is caused by the bacterium *Yersinia pestis* (abbreviated *Y. pestis*). Fleas bit rats infected with *Y. pestis* and then bit humans. The bacteria flowed in a person's bloodstream to the lymph nodes, then spread to the liver, spleen, and brain, destroying these organs. While the bubonic plague was spread mostly through the bite of infected fleas, it also passed directly from person to person through coughing or sneezing. This "pneumonic" or airborne

The port of Genoa, Italy, in the fifteenth century. The Black Death was carried here by rats that stowed away on ships coming from the Far East.

form of the plague spread rapidly, particularly in crowded cities.

The bubonic plague had originated in Mongolia, a region in eastern Asia. Changes in the climate forced Turkish and Mongolian nomads into new areas in search of food and water. Black rats found refuge in the nomads' caravans, traveling with them westward through India, into the Crimea region of eastern Europe, and to northern ports on the Black Sea, where Italian merchants had established trading colonies. With the rats went the plague, leaving behind a wide swath of death. According to some estimates, half the population of China fell victim to the plague during the thirteenth and fourteenth centuries.

In 1345, the plague struck Kaffa, a major trading city on the Black Sea. The citizens were baffled and afraid. No one could figure out the cause of this deadly disease. At the time, the Muslim citizens of Caffa were fighting Christian traders from Italy who had come to buy spices and silk that had been carried overland from Asia. According to one historian, the citizens of Caffa enlisted the aid of a local ruler, Janibeg, to fight the Christian merchants. When the merchants discovered that they were about to be attacked, they fled to a walled fortress in Caffa. They would have been defenseless against Janibeg's army had it not been for the plague—that relentless and nondiscriminating killer. The Black Death struck Janibeg's men as they lay siege to the fortress. In an angry final attack, Janibeg ordered his remaining men to catapult the dead bodies of soldiers over the walls of the fortress where the Italians were hiding.

The merchants fled to their ships to sail home, carrying with them the black rats and the plague. By the time the fleets reached Italy, most of the merchants and sailors were dead or dying. Some ships never made it home—everyone on board died, leaving the ships adrift at sea.

When Italian officials realized that the sailors and merchants were bringing disease to their cities, they ordered the men to remain on board in a quarantine—the enforced isolation of sick people to prevent the spread of a disease. But the rats did not heed the quarantine. They scurried down the docking ropes and brought infected fleas into the cities. The Black Death spread quickly. During the next two years, it moved northward through Europe and across the English Channel to Britain.

In Europe in the mid-1300s, life was difficult. For years, the winters had been harsh, the summers wet and cold. Crop failures and famine were common across the continent. In the countryside, peasants lived in shacks with dirt floors and straw-thatch roofs. They often shared their homes with their farm animals. By doing that, they risked getting animal-borne diseases, such as tuberculosis, influenza, and measles. The cities were crowded and filthy. Inside city walls, houses were tightly packed along dark, narrow streets. Garbage and human waste were thrown into open ditches, which flowed into rivers and streams. Bathing was considered dangerous. Vermin—rodents and insects—were an accepted part of city life.

People who lived in medieval times were no strangers to disease and famine. They were used to fatal and crippling diseases, including leprosy, typhus, smallpox, yellow fever, and malaria. But the Black Death was the most frightening. It struck Europe with tremendous force, condemning both rich and poor. Few people lived more than a week after being struck with the plague. With the pneumonic form of the disease, someone could be healthy in the morning and dead by nightfall.

Neighbors and friends fled from plague victims. Parents even abandoned their children. Victims often had a fever so high that they became delirious. They would shout and gyrate crazily in a final dance people called the "dance of death." As the victims died, foul-smelling fluids—sweat, excrement, and saliva—flowed from their bodies. The stench was overwhelming.

Crops were left to rot in the fields. Farm animals, left alone by owners who had either fled or died, wandered the countryside. Wolves entered towns and cities and fought over the corpses festering in the streets.

In England, William of Edynton, the bishop of Winchester, described the disaster: "The plague kills more viciously than a two-edged sword. Nobody dares enter any town, castle or village where it has struck. Everyone flees them in terror as they would the lair of a savage beast. There is an awful silence in such places; no merry music, no laughter. They have become dens of horror, like a wilderness. Where the countryside was fertile, it has now become a barren desert, for there is no one to plow the fields."

While some people believed the plague was a punishment from God for man's sins, others blamed Jewish people, who were a minority in central Europe. Thousands of Jews were burned alive by hordes seeking vengeance for the Black Death.

Within two years of its arrival in Italy, the bubonic plague had killed over 20 percent of the population of Europe. By the time it had run its course, four years after it arrived, 30 percent of the people were dead. Then the plague became dormant, or

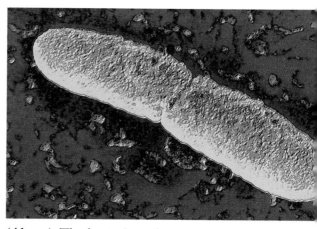

(Above) *The bacterium that causes bubonic plague,* Yersinia pestis, *shown magnified to 12,000 times its actual size*

(Left) *Alexandre Yersin discovered* Yersinia pestis, *which bears his name.*

inactive, for a decade, only to resurface. Until well into the 1400s, the Black Death reappeared about every 10 years, changing the Western world forever. After that, outbreaks of the plague happened less frequently and became more isolated.

As a result of the plague, entire cultures had to be rebuilt. The feudal system—in which wealthy landowners lived off the labor of their vassals, or serfs—began to crumble. On the other hand, land that had been too heavily farmed got the chance to lie fallow and become fertile again. New trees grew in forests that had been depleted. The cultural reawakening known as the Renaissance brought new ideas to the world.

In 1665, the bubonic plague returned with a vengeance, surfacing in London, England. Over one hundred thousand people died. Just when it seemed that nothing could be worse, a fire started in a baker's shop and quickly set the city ablaze. For five days, the fire raged. When it was over, the heart of London was reduced to ashes. But this tragedy had a bright side. The fire also destroyed the nests of the rats that carried the plague. After the Great Fire of London, the plague ended.

Soon afterward, the bubonic plague disappeared from most of Europe, although it continued to devastate some areas of Russia, Egypt, and Asia during the next three hundred years. In Europe, the effective enforcement of quarantines, better housing, and better sanitation helped stop the plague. Some historians suggest that the increased population of gray rats, which do not carry the plague bacteria, helped reduce its spread.

The plague is still around. From time to time, a case appears, but bubonic plague is no longer a major epidemic in developed countries. Correctly diagnosed, it can be treated with an antibiotic drug. The spread of the disease can be prevented by rodent control and good hygiene practices.

SMALLPOX

Over the centuries, smallpox epidemics have also ravaged many countries around the world. Smallpox is caused by a virus that spreads from person to person, by touch or through breathing or coughing. The earliest recorded case of smallpox occurred in 1157 B.C., when an Egyptian pharaoh named Ramses V was believed to have died of the disease.

Different strains of the virus produced different responses. Some cases were mild, while others were as deadly as the Black Death. The worst form of smallpox caused intense pain, high fever, and chills. Victims broke out in red, pus-filled sores, and their hands and feet swelled up. Skin fell away in strips, leaving the foul smell of rotting flesh. Large sores on victims' faces and backs bled, and their internal organs were damaged. Victims who did not die of smallpox were often sick for over a month. They were left with deep scars called pockmarks on their skin. Many victims lost their sight. But those who recovered were immune to, or protected against, smallpox forever.

Smallpox epidemics erupted in Asia, India, and Europe throughout the Middle Ages and into the early 1800s. Because people who survived smallpox were immune afterwards, there were lulls between epidemics. Then a new generation of children who were not immune to the disease would fall prey. In 1438 when smallpox swept through Paris, France, 50,000 people died—most of whom were children under age 12.

The most devastating impact of smallpox came with the European invasion of the Americas. When the Spanish conquistadors arrived in Central America in the early 1500s, they carried with them the smallpox virus, to which the native people had never been exposed. Because they had no immunity, the death toll was disastrous. In 1521, the disease spread through

Tenochtitlán, the Aztec capital of Mexico. Spanish soldiers, led by Cortés, easily defeated the superior forces of the Aztec army because the Aztec warriors were dying of smallpox.

Throughout Mexico and Central America, village after village was destroyed by smallpox. Bodies lay in the fields and piled up in houses. The same thing happened in Brazil when Portuguese colonists brought smallpox to South America.

In the early 1600s, English, French, and Dutch colonists arrived in North America. They, too, brought smallpox. The epidemic began in the Northeast and spread across the continent. Increase Mather, a Puritan leader, argued that God was clearly an Englishman, because the Indians died while the colonists did not. But Mather knew nothing about immunity.

In 1796, an English doctor named Edward Jenner observed that people who worked with cows often got a mild disease called cowpox. These people were not affected by smallpox— they were immune to it. He guessed that cowpox was a close cousin of smallpox, and that a person who received a small dose of cowpox would be protected from smallpox. He tried a risky experiment—one that would be considered highly unethical in modern times—to test his idea. He stuck a needle into the pus of a cowpox sore and then scratched the cowpox fluid into the skin of a healthy young boy, James Phipps. Several weeks later, Dr. Jenner injected Phipps with the watery pus from a smallpox sore. Phipps did not catch smallpox. He was immune. Jenner called the procedure *vaccina,* from *vacca,* the Latin word for cow. These vaccinations, or inoculations, with cowpox gave people immunity to smallpox. The battle against smallpox had begun.

The principle of immunity is the basis for all vaccinations. The human immune system uses proteins called antibodies. When these proteins meet an invading germ, they attack it.

In 1915 this young boy suffered from the devastating effects of smallpox, including the characteristic sores.

After the first attack, the body stores information about that invader, and if the same kind of microbe invades the body a second time, the antibodies will attack and destroy the invader immediately—before it can reproduce and cause a disease. If you receive a vaccination for mumps, you are given a very small dose of the mumps virus. Your body's antibodies destroy the virus. Your body will then remember the mumps virus, and if it ever invades again, the newly programmed antibodies will attack and destroy it before you even know you've been invaded. There are two types of vaccines. Some use live attenuated, or weakened, virus (mumps, measles, rubella) and others use inactivated, or killed, virus (influenza, hepatitis A and B). Sometimes vaccinations cause side effects or an allergic reaction. When you receive a vaccination, you will probably be warned about possible side effects, such as a slight fever or tenderness where you were vaccinated.

By the early 1900s, many countries had completely eliminated smallpox by enforced use of vaccines. In 1958, at a meeting of the World Health Organization, representatives of the Soviet Union suggested that WHO should organize a worldwide, cooperative effort to eradicate, or wipe out, smallpox.

The English physician Edward Jenner, who lived from 1749 to 1823, developed the first vaccine for smallpox.

A program to accomplish this seemingly overwhelming task was developed by Donald Henderson, a doctor from the United States. In 1967, he assembled a team and began the task of eradicating smallpox where it still existed. Under his plan, when an outbreak of smallpox was reported, doctors from WHO would travel to the site. There, they would verify that the disease was indeed smallpox, quarantine the area, and vaccinate all quarantined individuals to prevent new cases of the disease.

Once organized, the effort required the services of thousands of workers around the world and cost more than three hundred million dollars. Most of the doctors and scientists who undertook this heroic and often dangerous task were young people fresh out of medical school. In November 1975, Dr. Henderson reported that what was believed to be the last case of smallpox had been found in a little girl in Bangladesh. She survived the disease.

But the battle was not quite over. In February 1977, soon after Dr. Henderson retired, smallpox appeared in Somalia. This created a major problem. The area was in the middle of a war with the neighboring nation of Ethiopia. Refugees were fleeing the city of Ogaden, which was claimed by both Somalian and Ethiopian forces. Henderson's replacement on the smallpox project was a Japanese doctor named Isao Arita. Dr. Arita knew that by the end of the year, thousands of Somalian Muslims would celebrate the religious observance called *hajj* by making a pilgrimage to Mecca, Saudi Arabia. In Mecca, over two million worshipers would gather. If just a few people infected with smallpox mingled in that crowd, all efforts to eliminate the disease would be lost for at least another decade—maybe forever.

Dr. Arita was determined. His teams pressed forward in search of smallpox victims, trying to beat the hajj deadline. The war continued. The rainy season came, and mud flows blocked

Smallpox: The Ongoing Debate

Not long after smallpox was wiped out and the remaining stocks of the virus were securely stored, scientists from the World Health Organization began to discuss the possibility of destroying those samples. During the 1980s, virologists, or scientists who study viruses, recommended that the virus be destroyed after scientists determined its genetic blueprint. A date was set for the virus to be destroyed, but not everyone agreed with this plan. For years, scientists have been debating whether or not to keep the virus.

Those who favor destroying the virus fear that if the virus got out into the public through an accident or a terrorist act, smallpox would devastate populations that have no immunity to the disease and have not been vaccinated against it. Other scientists say that the virus should be preserved, because it may provide important information for studying new or emerging viruses. They argue that the virus will help in formulating vaccines and developing drugs to combat other viruses.

The situation became more complicated when cases of a related disease, monkeypox, increased. Since February 1996, there have been more than eight hundred suspected cases of human monkeypox reported from the Democratic Republic of the Congo (formerly Zaire), in central Africa. Like smallpox, monkeypox can be fatal, though it usually is not.

The smallpox vaccine has been found to be effective against monkeypox. Although WHO has a supply of smallpox vaccine, scientists decided not to use the vaccine because of the high incidence of AIDS in the Democratic Republic of the Congo. A smallpox vaccination could be fatal to a person whose immune system has already been weakened by AIDS.

Some people believe that the emergence of a disease such as monkeypox strengthens the argument in favor of preserving the smallpox virus. In 1999, WHO voted to hold off on destroying the stocks of smallpox until 2004.

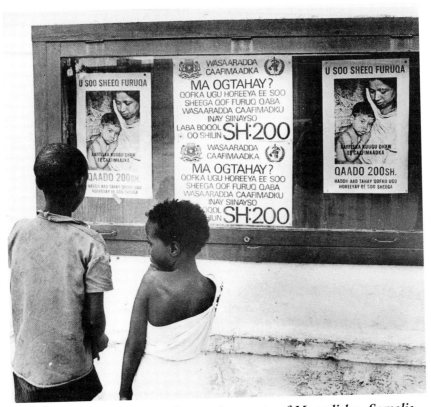

In the late 1970s, posters all over the streets of Mogadishu, Somalia, offered a reward equal to 33 dollars to anyone who reported a small-pox case.

roads. But the doctors did not give up. They drove through the rain and the muck. They asked questions and examined sick people. They vaccinated everyone they could find.

Finally, in the town of Merka, Somalia, they found a lean, wiry man named Ali Maow Maalin, who had the last known case of smallpox. They watched and waited. Maalin recovered and became immune. WHO doctors waited some more. No one else in Maalin's family or town, or anywhere in Somalia, came down with smallpox.

On May 8, 1980, WHO declared victory over smallpox. All traces of the disease had been eliminated. The only remaining samples of the virus were frozen in secure vaults at the CDC in Atlanta, Georgia, and at a similar center in Koltsovo, Russia.

ANTHRAX

Anthrax is primarily a disease of herbivorous (plant-eating) animals like cattle and sheep. Transmission to humans is usually related to those who farm the animals or work in the textile industry. Through history anthrax has been known by a number of different names including woolsorters' disease, ragpickers' disease, and the Siberian plague.

Since antiquity anthrax has existed in many parts of the world. The fifth of the ten plagues reported in the Old Testament of the Bible, in which all of Egypt's cattle died, may have been anthrax, according to Chester Drum, an anthrax researcher at the University of Chicago. The sixth plague, the plague of boils, may also have been anthrax, this time affecting humans. The worst anthrax outbreak in history was probably the Black Bane, an epidemic that spread through Europe in the 1600s. It resulted in the deaths of many thousands of humans and animals.

The disease is devastating to farm animals. Horses, oxen, cows, sheep, and goats stricken by anthrax fall behind the herd. An infected animal's head lowers, its breathing becomes heavy, and it quickly falls dead, often with its belly grotesquely swollen. The progress of the disease is so fast that herders and farmers can only watch helplessly as their animals die.

Until the end of the nineteenth century, people were at a loss to understand the cause of this terrible pestilence. Blame was placed on stagnant water, insects, overexposure to hot sun, deadly gases from marshes, or poisoned weeds. Some pastures were thought to have been cursed by sorcerers, because animals who grazed in these places died of anthrax.

In 1876, physician Robert Koch demonstrated that a rod-shaped bacterium, *Bacillus anthracis,* causes anthrax. Through his studies of *Bacillus anthracis,* Koch developed a series of steps that are still used to determine whether a particular bacterium causes a specific disease. These steps are called Koch's postulates.

In 1877, herds in central France were particularly hard hit by recurring outbreaks of anthrax. The French Minister of Agriculture called for help from Louis Pasteur, who had earlier in that century established that bacteria cause diseases. Pasteur knew that anthrax was caused by a bacterium, but fashioning a vaccine proved to be difficult. On August 18, 1878, he opened a laboratory near Chartres, France, with collaborators Charles Chamberland, August Vinsot, and Emile Roux. By 1881, they had developed a vaccine to protect the herds.

Bacillus anthracis lives naturally in certain types of soils. Hardy forms of the bacterium, called spores, can survive for years in soil or on contaminated objects. Animals are infected when they ingest spores while grazing, breathe in spores, or eat animals that died of anthrax. Once inside a host, the bacteria enter the blood or tissues, where they multiply and release deadly toxins (poisons) that cause the symptoms of the disease.

The occurrence of anthrax in humans has, historically, been limited. People generally are infected due to contact with infected animals or animal products such as wool or hides. In countries with effective public health programs, such as the

United States, human infection is rare. The disease has become important as a threat to humans in the United States only because of its potential as a weapon of bioterrorism.

In people, anthrax occurs in three forms: cutaneous (affecting the skin), intestinal (intestines), and inhalation (lungs). At least 95 percent of all cases of anthrax are the cutaneous form.

Cutaneous anthrax occurs when bacteria enter the body through a break in the skin. The disease begins as an itchy bump that develops into a painless ulcer with a black center. Cutaneous anthrax is easily diagnosed and cured.

Intestinal anthrax results from eating undercooked meat from anthrax-infected animals. It is seldom seen in America because of thorough inspection of livestock. The symptoms include nausea, loss of appetite, vomiting, and fever, followed by abdominal pain, vomiting of blood, and severe diarrhea. Without treatment, the disease can be fatal.

Inhalation anthrax, caused by breathing in anthrax spores, is rare. This form is the most dangerous. From the lungs, spores quickly reach the bloodstream, where they multiply rapidly. The disease progresses swiftly, so early diagnosis and treatment are critical. Early symptoms resemble those of flu, with sudden fever, difficulty breathing, and sweating. In the final stages the patient develops severe breathing problems and goes into shock. The skin turns bluish. Death can follow in just a few hours.

Early treatment of anthrax is important, but diagnosis of the inhalation and intestinal forms can be difficult. Anthrax is diagnosed by isolating *Bacillus anthracis* from the blood, skin ulcers, or lung secretions, or by measuring specific antibodies in the blood. The disease is treated with antibiotics.

Chapter Four

FROM THE TROPICS TO THE TUNDRA:
MALARIA, INFLUENZA, AND DIPHTHERIA

Major infectious diseases have continued to ravage communities and countries into modern times. Vaccines, antibiotics, and other medicines have helped reduce the danger, but infectious diseases still challenge physicians' and scientists' skills and knowledge. Malaria, influenza, and diphtheria are diseases that have pushed people to dramatic feats.

A DEADLY MOSQUITO BITE

Malaria is a disease that occurs in tropical and subtropical regions of the world. It is spread by the bite of female mosquitoes—not just any mosquito, but certain species of *Anopheles* mosquitoes. Malaria is not the only disease borne by mosquitoes. Yellow fever, dengue fever, and encephalitis are other major diseases carried by mosquitoes.

Malaria transmission happens in three basic stages. First, a female mosquito bites a human, sucking in the person's blood. If the human has malaria, then his or her blood contains *Plasmodium* parasites—the cause of malaria. These parasites enter the mosquito with the person's blood and flow to the mosquito's stomach, where they reproduce. When the

Doctors, army officers, and reporters donned surgical gowns and masks in a 1918 tour of hospitals to observe the treatment of Spanish flu patients.

mosquito bites another human, the parasites are transferred into the human's blood. In the person's bloodstream, the parasites are carried into the liver, where they reproduce and invade red blood cells. Eventually the parasites cause the red blood cells to burst, sending more parasites into the bloodstream to start the cycle again. During these periods when parasites flood the bloodstream, the person has bouts of fever and may die.

Over the centuries, malaria has sickened and killed millions of people. Malaria causes fever, chills, nausea, muscle and joint pain, weakness, vomiting, and sometimes convulsions or coma. In the United States, malaria was a serious problem until the mid-1930s. By 1950, thanks to effective mosquito control, improved medicines, and a higher standard of living, the disease had been almost completely eliminated in the United States. Malaria is still widespread in Central and South America, Africa, Southeast Asia, India, and Indonesia.

In the past, many people believed that malaria was caused by bad air—the word *malaria* means "bad air" in Italian. They thought that unhealthy vapors, or miasmas, came from swamps, low-lying lands, and bogs. Although some cultures in East Africa had long attributed malaria to mosquito bites, most European scientists and physicians dismissed this notion as folklore.

In 1807, Dr. John Crawford of Baltimore, Maryland, was ridiculed for publishing a paper that suggested malaria could be transmitted when mosquitoes laid their eggs in humans. Ninety years later, he was proved to be closer to the truth than those who had laughed at his idea.

In 1884, a French army doctor named Charles Laveran, who was serving in Algeria, began examining droplets of blood taken from French soldiers who had malaria. He noticed that

(Left) *A false-color scanning electron micrograph of the stomach wall of a mosquito infected with malarial parasites (the round blue objects). The parasites are in an early stage in their life cycle.*

(Above) *A female anopheles mosquito*

malaria patients' blood contained more red blood cells than healthy blood contained. He was even more mystified by something that happened as he watched the blood under the glass of his microscope. Sometimes the red blood cells would expand and swell and finally burst open, releasing malaria-causing parasites. But many scientists of the time doubted the validity of Dr. Laveran's discovery.

At about the same time, Dr. Patrick Manson, an English physician working in India, developed the hypothesis that mosquitoes were the likely carriers of malaria. This hypothesis was an inspired guess that Dr. Manson arrived at by looking for a common association between the disease and the environment. He observed that malaria appeared in areas with a warm climate and swampy lands. In these areas, the most common insect was the mosquito, which bit humans.

This was a good start, but not a definite link. Later, an English scientist-poet, Ronald Ross, put the theories of Dr. Laveran and Dr. Manson to a scientific test. Ross had invented

Sir Ronald Ross, who lived from 1857 to 1932, discovered that plasmodium parasites reproduce in the stomach of female anopheles mosquitoes.

a portable microscope, which he carried with him on his assignment to a British regiment in India. There, he began a painstaking quest to isolate in mosquitoes the same parasite that Dr. Laveran had seen in malaria patients' blood. He corresponded with Dr. Manson and studied the work of Dr. Laveran as he pursued his investigation.

Ross collected mosquitoes and persuaded "volunteers" who had malaria to let these mosquitoes bite them. Using pins for tools, Ross dissected the mosquitoes and examined them under his portable microscope, looking for the plasmodium parasites. For two years, Ross pursued his research without success. The problem was that he was looking at the wrong mosquitoes. He did not know that only certain kinds of mosquitoes carry malaria.

In Sigur Ghat, a valley in India where coffee plantations thrived, Ross finally found his answer. There he identified anopheles mosquitoes. When he examined these insects, he found plasmodia. In 1898, he observed that the plasmodium parasites reproduced in the mosquito's stomach, then entered the saliva. This was the way the parasite traveled from mosquito to human.

CONTROLLING MALARIA

In 1881, a French company launched an effort to build a canal that would connect the Atlantic Ocean with the Pacific Ocean across the narrow Isthmus of Panama. The company was defeated, not by the enormity of the task, but by malaria-carrying mosquitoes. One writer reported that because of the mosquitoes, only 20 percent of the workers who came to Panama remained for more than two months, and those who did stay were often so weakened by malaria that they could not work.

Yellow Fever
and the Louisiana Purchase

Another disease carried by mosquitoes is yellow fever. The virus that causes yellow fever is carried by female *Aedes aegypti* mosquitoes, which get the virus from monkeys. The virus lives in monkeys without causing illness. When an infected mosquito bites a human, the virus passes with the mosquito's saliva into the person's bloodstream.

A. aegypti mosquitoes prefer to lay their eggs in containers of clean water. They often lay eggs in cups and pots where rainwater collects. These mosquitoes are as likely to breed in cities and towns as in swamps.

Yellow fever may have spread to the Americas by mosquitoes breeding in the ships sailing with Columbus in 1492. The disease wiped out entire populations in the Caribbean, paving the way for European conquests.

In 1802, Napoleon Bonaparte, the emperor of France, sent 33,000 soldiers to French-ruled Haiti, located on an island in the Caribbean Sea, to stop a revolt by slaves led by Toussaint L'Ouverture. But yellow fever struck down over 85 percent of Napoleon's army. This left the Haitians, most of whom were immune to yellow fever, to control their own nation.

The devastation wrought by yellow fever undoubtedly helped persuade Napoleon that land in the New World was not worth the taking. Consequently, in 1803, he was ready to deal with U.S. president Thomas Jefferson and sell the Louisiana Territory to the United States in a deal known as the Louisiana Purchase.

After eight years of attempts and failure, the French company gave up, and the United States bought the rights to build the canal. President Theodore Roosevelt assigned Colonel William C. Gorgas, an army doctor, the task of destroying the mosquitoes that caused malaria and yellow fever.

For two years, Col. Gorgas commanded his forces to drain swamps and dry up places where water might collect. The soldiers also cleared weeds and covered mosquito breeding areas with a solution of carbolic acid, resin, and caustic soda. Their mission was to eliminate any area where mosquitoes could breed. They also built screens around the shacks where workers lived, and Col. Gorgas hired additional laborers for 10 cents an

A worker applies poison in an attempt to control the spread of mosquitoes during the construction of the Panama Canal.

hour to stay in the living quarters and swat or capture mosquitoes. Gorgas's campaign succeeded in reducing the mosquito population. In turn, the incidence of yellow fever and malaria dropped, and the Panama Canal was completed in 1914.

Twenty-seven years later, after Japanese forces bombed Pearl Harbor, Hawaii, in 1941, American military leaders saw a need to establish year-round training bases in southern states for the U.S. armed forces. To do this, they had to deal with malaria, which was still a problem in the South. The surgeon general of the United States, Thomas Parran, created the National Defense Malaria Control Activities office to tackle the issue. The office was headquartered in Atlanta, Georgia, because the large Okefenokee swamp in southeastern Georgia provided an ideal breeding ground for mosquitoes.

The malaria office opened on Peachtree Street in Atlanta. Very quickly, more than four thousand mosquito warriors began spraying DDT pesticide, Paris Green, and diesel oil on every suspected breeding place. They covered Puerto Rico, the Virgin Islands, and the southern United States from Florida to California. This concentrated effort virtually eliminated malaria in the United States. But the malaria office did not close its doors—it began to deal with other diseases and ultimately became the Centers for Disease Control and Prevention.

TREATING MALARIA

For centuries, the only known treatment for malaria was quinine. Quinine contains a compound called quinoline, which is found in the bark of the cinchona tree. Quinoline kills the plasmodium parasite. In the early 1600s, Jesuit missionaries traveling in South America learned of the curative powers of the bark of the cinchona tree and brought it to Europe.

Two hundred years later, Charles Ledger, an English adventurer, wandered through the mountains and forests of Peru, looking for valuable quinine-producing cinchona trees. He succeeded, and he gathered seeds from the trees to take back to England. He believed that with these seeds, he would become honored and wealthy. But the British government did not recognize the value of his find. Ledger was disappointed but determined. He approached several governments in Europe, offering to sell the seeds of trees that had the power to cure malaria. He finally found a country that was interested. The Dutch government appreciated the importance of the cinchona tree and the value of the seeds. Dutch officials purchased Ledger's seeds and began planting cinchona plantations on the island of Java, a Dutch colony in Indonesia. Ledger received a salary for life, and the scientific name of the cinchona tree— *Cinchona ledgeriana*—bears his name.

Until World War II, the Dutch government maintained a monopoly on naturally grown quinine. During this war, however, the Japanese military gained control of the cinchona plantations in the Dutch East Indies (Indonesia), hoping that this move would cripple American forces. These islands provided the principal source for quinine, since the cinchona trees in South America had died in the mid-1800s. The Japanese reasoned that the Americans could not do battle in the mosquito-infested islands of the South Pacific without quinine for the soldiers.

More than five hundred thousand American servicemen did suffer from malaria during the battles in the South Pacific. But the widespread use of DDT to kill mosquitoes and the development of quinacrine, a synthetic substitute for quinine, took away the Japanese army's advantage.

The modern medicines chloroquine and primaquine have been able to cure most cases of malaria. Mosquito control also reduces malaria outbreaks. But the war against malaria is far from won. Emerging parasites have become resistant to chloroquine and primaquine. Some new breeds of mosquitoes are resistant to DDT and other insecticides. A second battle against malaria has begun.

Although malaria is no longer a threatening disease in the United States, it is still a major threat in many places in the world. Forty percent of the world's people live in regions where malaria is a problem. It is estimated that more than 350 million new cases of malaria occur worldwide each year, and approximately 2 million people a year die of the disease.

THE SPANISH FLU EPIDEMIC

Every fall, state health departments make announcements about that season's flu shot. If you wonder why you may need a new flu shot each year, it's because influenza—the flu—is caused by a virus that is very unstable. It changes into new strains all the time. The flu virus is a sphere with little peaks or spikes sticking out. Each year, new strains of flu emerge, and each strain (usually named for the place it was first detected) is slightly different. Because of the continuous changes, any particular flu vaccine will not be effective against another strain of flu.

The worst epidemic ever to strike the United States was the influenza outbreak of 1918, called the Spanish flu. It swept across America and around the world, becoming a pandemic. Normally, influenza is not deadly to healthy young people, although it can be fatal to older people or people who suffer

(Left) *A computer graphic illustrates an influenza virus at 250,000 times its actual size.*

(Right) *Influenza viruses (the tiny yellow spheres) have invaded this cell. Like other viruses, flu viruses take control of the cell and turn the nucleus (light red) into a factory for producing more viruses.*

other serious ailments. But the Spanish flu swiftly killed healthy young men and women.

It first appeared on March 11, 1918, at Fort Riley, Kansas, where nearly one hundred soldiers suddenly became ill on the same day. From Kansas, the virus traveled with the soldiers overseas to the battlefields of Europe, where World War I was being fought. The virus passed from man to man in wet, muddy trenches, in the crowded barracks, and on troop ships. Some soldiers died from this terrible flu. Others brought it back to their home countries, traveling by ship or train across the world.

The German soldiers called the flu the Blitz Katarrh, while English soldiers called it "Flanders grippe." The American soldiers, mistakenly believing that the illness had come from Spain, called it "Spanish flu" or "Spanish lady."

The Spanish flu reached around the world, from the tropics to the poles. Over 20 million people around the world died, including more than five hundred thousand Americans. Ten times as many people died at home in the United States from the flu as died in combat in World War I. Many victims died of a bacterial pneumonia brought on by the flu, but most died of the flu itself.

Illness and death were everywhere. Businesses slowed down or stopped. Schools, movie theaters, and other public places were closed because so many people were sick. People wore face masks to halt the spread of the flu germ.

In San Francisco, California, public health officials passed an ordinance forbidding anyone from appearing in public without a face mask. At the University of Michigan at Ann Arbor, any student caught without a mask was automatically suspended. In some cities, streetcar conductors refused to allow passengers to ride without a face mask. A town in Arizona passed a law forbidding people from shaking hands.

The epidemic spread during the summer of 1918, reaching its peak in the fall. Then it waned, reappeared in 1919, and finally disappeared as mysteriously as it had begun. At the time of the epidemic, no one knew what was causing it. Researchers attempted to isolate and identify the microbe. It wasn't found until the mid-1930s, when Dr. Richard Shope found the biological mixture that had proved so destructive. He suggested that the flu was caused by a combination of a virus and a bacterium, Pfeiffer's bacillus, found in pigs. Dr. Shope believed that when these microbes moved from pigs to humans, they caused a deadly combination of viral flu (called swine flu) and bacterial pneumonia. Some physicians haven't accepted this theory, however.

Many microbes live only in certain animals and do not infect humans. Some of these microbes are harmless to the animal— they do not cause disease in the animal. Other microbes cause disease in animals, but not humans. But sometimes microbes mutate, and then they can jump from an animal to a human. To mutate means that some part of an organism's molecular structure changes. Viruses that do not change to meet new conditions will not survive, while viruses that do mutate may live.

When viruses or bacteria mutate, a disease that had previously affected only animals may move into a human host. This can happen when people live close to animals, as farmers do, or when humans invade a microbe's natural habitat such as by clearing jungles to build farms and towns. The Spanish flu epidemic was thought to be caused by a virus that had mutated and jumped from pigs to humans.

Fifty years later, few U.S. citizens remembered the horrors of the Spanish flu. But epidemiologists did remember. In January 1976, Dr. Martin Goldfield, the chief of epidemiology for the state of New Jersey, recognized a swine flu-type virus in blood taken from a soldier who had died from influenza at Fort Dix, New Jersey. Alarmed, Dr. Goldfield promptly sent samples to the CDC in Atlanta.

By the 1970s, doctors knew that the 1918 flu virus had jumped from pigs to humans and then spread from human to human. While a milder variety of swine flu had been known to infect farmers who raised hogs, this case of influenza—in a soldier who had had no contact with pigs—suggested human-to-human transmission.

At the urging of doctors at the CDC, the U.S. government

initiated a massive drive to manufacture and distribute a vaccine to protect millions of citizens against swine flu in order to prevent an epidemic. Over 40 million shots were administered in October and November 1976. But this was the epidemic that never was. Wherever the virus had come from to kill the soldier at Fort Dix, it no longer seemed to exist. For almost a year, no more cases of swine flu appeared. But a new problem developed.

Cases of Guillain-Barré syndrome, a rare paralytic disease, began to occur a few weeks after the swine flu inoculation program began. Some physicians worried that the number of cases was high enough to raise the question of whether the disease had any relationship to the mass vaccination program administered

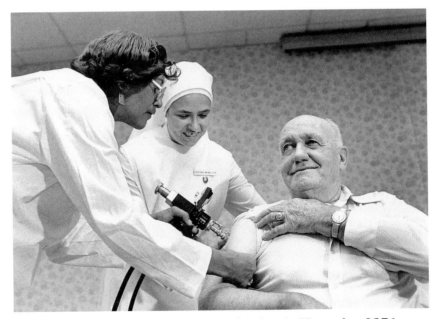

A man in Chicago receives the swine flu shot in November 1976.

during the fall of 1976. Flu vaccinations do carry a slight possibility of side effects, such as pain and swelling at the spot where the shot is injected, a slight fever, or a mild case of the flu. On rare occasions, a more serious reaction will occur.

The doctors needed a baseline, a measurement of the normal incidence of Guillain-Barré syndrome in the population over a given period of time. This would help them determine if the current number of cases was higher than usual. The doctors turned to the Mayo Clinic for help. Dr. Leonard Kurland, chief of epidemiology, had the answer. By looking at the normally occurring incidence of the disease, as measured by the clinic's extensive population records, Dr. Kurland could calculate whether there might have been an increase in Guillain-Barré following the vaccinations. The answer was yes.

The initial epidemiological information suggested that the occurrence of this disease had increased seven times. No one knew then or knows yet the actual cause of this form of paralysis. But health officials were disturbed by the new information. Health officials from around the country discussed the situation and decided to end the swine flu vaccination program immediately. Within 10 weeks, the number of newly reported Guillain-Barré cases fell back to normal levels.

When a mysterious flu virus struck chickens in Hong Kong in 1997, epidemiologists wondered if this virus could jump from birds to people, as the swine flu had moved from pigs to humans. In December 1997, 18 cases of this new flu appeared in people in Hong Kong. The government in Hong Kong ordered the killing of more than one million chickens, ducks, and geese to block any chance of transmitting the virus from birds to humans. By the end of January 1998, the threat had disappeared. No epidemic materialized.

A LIFE-OR-DEATH RACE IN ALASKA

Diphtheria is a contagious disease that causes a victim's throat to swell, cutting off his or her breathing. In the United States, diphtheria is prevented by the DPT vaccination (a combination of diphtheria, pertussis-whooping cough, and tetanus vaccines), which is given to young children. The diphtheria bacterium, *Corynebacterium diphtheriae,* produces a powerful poison called an exotoxin. A patient who is infected with diphtheria must receive an antitoxin—a serum that blocks the action of the poison. It has become standard to follow this with antibiotics. Without the antitoxin, victims are doomed to slow, painful suffocation.

Before diphtheria vaccinations became available in 1923, epidemics of this "malignant throat distemper" often swept through communities in colonial America. Most victims were children. Many historians believe that the first president of the United States, George Washington, died of diphtheria.

In 1925, the most dramatic diphtheria epidemic in U.S. history happened in Nome, Alaska, where the newly developed vaccine had not yet been introduced. During an average winter in Nome, temperatures often plunge to 20 degrees below zero. But in January 1925, a cold wind blowing eastward from the Bering Strait made the temperature drop even lower.

Nome was isolated from the rest of the world in the winter, and Dr. Curtis Welch was the only doctor in this city of two thousand citizens. On January 21, he was called to a home to see a sick child. The child had a high fever and a very sore throat. This was not unusual, but when Dr. Welch peered into the child's throat, he saw that it had turned from healthy red to white. A toxin was killing the cells lining the child's throat. This was diphtheria!

Corynebacterium diphtheriae, *the bacterium that causes diphtheria, produces a toxin causing inflammation of the throat and tonsils and damage to the heart and nervous system.*

Before the day was over, two more children came down with the same symptoms. Dr. Welch immediately recognized the potential for a deadly epidemic. He had no antitoxin, and none of the children in Nome had been vaccinated against diphtheria.

The doctor rushed to the telegraph office. The town's telegraph operator hurriedly tapped Dr. Welch's frantic plea to public health offices in Fairbanks and Anchorage, thousands of miles away. He needed antitoxin, and he needed it right away.

Telegraph lines around the country buzzed. Dr. J. B. Beeson at the Alaska Railroad Hospital in Anchorage had the needed units of antitoxin serum. (Serum is a fluid containing the anti-toxin.) The problem was, how would they get the serum to Nome? A railroad line ran north from Anchorage to Fairbanks, but the closest that it came to Nome was the station at Nenana, and that was still 675 miles away from Nome. No airplanes were available, and even if there were, the weather was turning bad. A winter storm was forming in the Bering Strait.

The governor of Alaska decided that the only reliable way to get the serum from Nenana to Nome was by dogsled, along the Iditarod Trail, one of several major winter routes. This trail, named for the town of Iditarod, was used primarily by dogsled mushers who carried supplies, mail, and a few passengers. By telegraph communication, relay teams of drivers and dogs were organized and assigned portions of the trail to cover.

Meanwhile, the first child died, and two others lay dying. Other cases of diphtheria broke out. Normally, the trip from Nenana to Nome took 20 days by dogsled. If this trip took that long, however, the serum would be too late.

Dr. Beeson carefully bottled the serum, wrapped it, and packed it. The 20-pound package was loaded on the train in Anchorage, and the train headed north to Nenana. At 11 P.M. on January 27, the train steamed into Nenana. The package was handed to William "Wild Bill" Shannon, who set out immediately into the dark of a long Alaskan winter night with 10 powerful husky dogs pulling his sled. The temperature had dropped to 30 below zero and the wind was rising.

While telegraph reports flashed the news to newspapers all around the United States, the race against the deadly diphtheria bacteria began. About 20 men and their dogs headed toward their assigned places along the trail. The men, sleds, and dogs carried the serum across the vast, snow-covered land, over the Yukon

River, and steadily westward toward Nome. At each stop—including Tolovana, Tanana, Nine Mile, Ruby, Whiskey Creek, Galena, Bishop Mountain, Old Woman, and Unalakleet—the next man was ready to take over his leg of the journey.

Charlie Evans was miles short of his destination of Nulato when his two lead sled dogs fell over dead. But Evans did not quit. He hooked the dogs' harnesses to himself and led his dogs onward, racing into the howling wind and bitter cold. The temperature was so cold that if a man lost his gloves, his hands would freeze in minutes.

Meanwhile, Leonhard Seppala, a renowned dog-racing champion who lived in Nome, hitched his dogs behind his lead dog, Togo, and headed east to meet the approaching dog teams. After traveling over 160 miles, with one stop at a friend's igloo, he picked up the serum at Shaktoolik and headed back toward Nome. The day before, he had made a dangerous crossing on the ice of Norton Bay. This direct route had saved one hundred miles of travel. Now he needed to recross the bay in a fierce wind. He knew that if the wind shifted, the ice could be blown out of the bay, carrying him, his dogs, his sled, and the serum out to sea. But time was running out for the children of Nome. Seppala did not hesitate. Eighty-six miles later, he reached the western shore of Norton Bay, just as the wind began pushing the ice pack out of the bay. Seppala stopped at a roadhouse in Golovin, where he collapsed for needed warmth, food, and rest. Charlie Olson took the serum and headed west.

The next 25 miles along the trail were the most difficult. The wind was now slicing directly across the trail, throwing the driver, sled, and dogs off the trail repeatedly. Olson pushed forward. He suffered severe frostbite, but he made it to the Bluff roadhouse, where he met the next driver, Gunnar Kaasen.

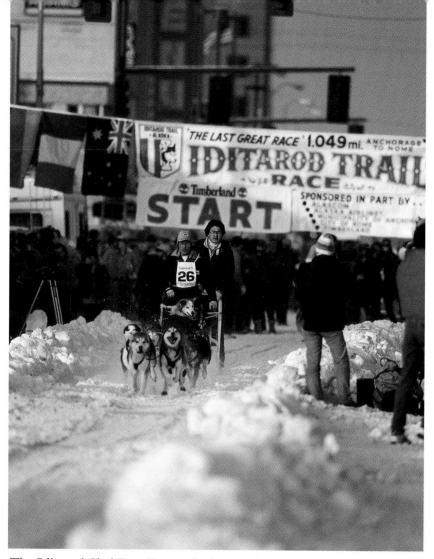

The Iditarod Sled Dog Race, which runs from Anchorage, Alaska, to Nome, Alaska, has been held every March since 1973.

The blizzard was intensifying. Kaasen was 53 miles from Nome, and Ed Rohn was racing to meet him for the final leg. In the blindness of the blizzard, however, the men did not meet, and Kaasen had no choice but to keep going. Suddenly, a powerful gust of wind blew his sled onto its side, tossing the package of serum into the snow. Frantically, Kaasen sifted through the whirling, twisting snow. Miraculously, he found the package.

He rushed on through the night, led by his lead husky, Balto. Totally blinded by the snow, Kaasen half rode and half ran as the powerful dogs pressed forward into the blizzard. Suddenly, the sound of the wind changed pitch. The wail of the wind softened. They were between the buildings of Nome. They had made it!

Inside the hospital, Dr. Welch heard a dog bark. He eased open the front door, which caught in the wind and jerked him out into the storm. There stood Gunnar Kaasen, his smile almost hidden beneath his fur hat and his beard layered with frost and snow. Kaasen held up both hands, cradling the precious cargo. The relay team had reached Nome in a record-setting five days, seven hours. By then 5 children had died, but another 29 were saved from terrible strangulation by diphtheria.

This amazing rescue is remembered each year during the annual Iditarod dogsled race in Alaska. And in Central Park, in the middle of Manhattan in New York City, a large bronze statue of an Alaskan husky named Balto honors the 20 drivers and 150 dogs who carried antitoxin serum to Nome in the winter of 1925.

Chapter Five

MODERN KILLERS:
LEGIONNAIRES' DISEASE, EBOLA, AND MUERTO CANYON VIRUS

In 1928, thanks to a serendipitous accident, a powerful new weapon was developed to help fight bacterial diseases. That year, a Scottish scientist named Alexander Fleming went off for a week on a vacation. Before he left, he had been growing a common type of bacteria, staphylococcus, in his laboratory. While he was gone, a mold (a form of fungus) floated through the air in the lab. A fleck of that mold landed in Fleming's culture of staph bacteria. Amazingly, where the mold landed, the bacteria died.

When Fleming returned from vacation and saw that the staphylococci had died near the mold, he immediately realized the significance of the observation. He used the mold, *Penicillium,* as the basis to create the "miracle drug" penicillin, which worked to stop many bacterial diseases.

Since then, antibiotics such as penicillin have been effective in fighting a wide range of bacterial diseases. Many people thought that with antibiotic drugs, humans had won the war against microbes. But that dream has been shattered as new epidemics have continued to arise with deadly force.

EPIDEMIC IN PHILADELPHIA

During the summer of 1976, while much of the United States celebrated the nation's bicentennial, medical experts debated

Legionnella pneumophila *bacteria cause the deadly Legionnaires' disease.*

whether the Spanish flu epidemic of 1918 would resurface as a swine flu epidemic that winter.

That summer in Philadelphia, Pennsylvania, where the Declaration of Independence had been signed two hundred years earlier, members of the American Legion, the country's largest veterans' organization, attended a convention. Hundreds of Legionnaires and their wives attended meetings and banquets and partied at four hotels in the City of Brotherly Love.

It was mid-July and hot. Suddenly, two men fell ill with high fever, aching muscles, and pneumonia. These cases were followed by many more. All the victims were men and women who had attended the Legionnaires' convention. By August 2, 8 people were dead and 150 were ill. Before it was over, 29 people died from the swiftly striking acute form of pneumonia.

Was it the dreaded swine flu? With all the attention that had been given to the threat of an epidemic, many people believed the flu had struck again.

Doctors rushed tissue and blood samples from the patients to the CDC. Within a day, the scientists had ruled out influenza viruses as the cause. It was not swine flu. Labeled by the media as "Legionnaire killer" and "killer pneumonia," the outbreak caused public panic. What was this epidemic?

Dr. David Fraser, an experienced epidemiologist, was sent from Atlanta to lead the investigation. His team questioned hundreds of Legionnaires and their families. The medical detectives were looking for the one thing all these people had in common. They knew that all the victims had attended the convention, but that was not enough. Many people who had attended had not gotten sick. The epidemiologists asked detailed questions. Who got the disease—old or young people, men or women? When did they arrive? How did they travel?

An outbreak of Legionnaires' disease occurred at the Bellevue Stratford Hotel in Philadelphia in July 1976.

What, when, and where did they eat? Where did they go while they were in Philadelphia? Where did they stay?

The detective work paid off. The epidemiologists analyzed their data to find the common denominator among those who had fallen ill. Although all the Legionnaires had attended the convention, they had not all stayed at the same hotel. The one thing those who became ill had in common was that they had all stayed at the Bellevue Stratford Hotel, a famous old hotel in the heart of Philadelphia.

With that important fact determined, the search began for a

microbe or toxic chemical that could have caused the outbreak. Back in Atlanta, microbiologist Dr. Joseph McDade and physician-scientist Dr. Charles "Shep" Shepard tried every test they could think of on the blood samples from people who had gotten the disease. But they couldn't find a chemical or microbe that would account for the symptoms. Although the scientists suspected a microbe rather than a chemical had caused the outbreak, they could not isolate a bacterium or virus in the blood samples. No microbes showed up in the ordinary culture. The doctors tried different nutrients as a culture. Finally, when they used untreated eggs as a culture, they succeeded. A new bacterium grew this time.

By January 1977, the CDC epidemiologists had found the culprit—a bacterium they called *Legionnella pneumophila*. They also made another discovery. When they examined blood samples from several previous unsolved cases of disease—outbreaks of pneumonia in Washington, D.C., in 1965, and in Pontiac, Michigan, in 1968—these samples contained *Legionnella* bacteria.

Legionnella bacteria normally lie dormant in puddles of water. Air-conditioning towers, such as the one at the Bellevue Stratford, provide a perfect breeding ground for them. The bacteria had traveled in airborne water droplets through the hotel's air-conditioning ducts to find warm hosts in the guests and hotel workers who breathed in the microbes.

Since then, smaller outbreaks of Legionnaires' disease have been reported, and *Legionnella* bacteria have been found in shower heads and water faucet pipes. Hot tubs, humidifiers, and decorative fountains can also harbor these and other bacteria. Fortunately, Legionnaires' disease cannot spread from person to person.

A Deadly Virus from the Jungle

In September 1976, not long after the Legionnaires fell sick in Philadelphia, an outbreak occurred on the other side of the world. In northern Zaire (since renamed the Democratic Republic of the Congo), a country in central Africa, a young man received an injection of medicine at the small Yambuku Mission Hospital. The village of Yambuku is in the Bumba Zone, an area of rain forests near the Ebola River. Local people suffering from malaria would come to the hospital in Yambuku to get shots of medicine to ease their chills and pains. Because the hospital staff had little money to buy supplies, they used the same few unsterilized needles to inject hundreds of patients.

A couple of days after the young man, who taught at the local school, received his injection, he became ill again. First he had a headache. Then he began to sweat from a fever, and the joints of his arms and legs ached. As the days passed, he rapidly grew sicker. A rash appeared on his face, then all over his body. He began to shake and tremble. The red spots on his body turned to large blotches, then bruises. The teacher's skin became soft and pulpy, and chunks of it fell off his body. Blood oozed from his mouth and he vomited a black, slippery substance. His insides were being turned into a slimy jelly. Blood flowed from his eyes as he went into a seizure. His body twitched and his arms and legs thrashed. After three days, he died. He was the first victim of one of the deadliest diseases in the world—Ebola hemorrhagic fever.

Shortly after the teacher's death, 13 of the 17 staff workers at the clinic died in the same way. One of the nuns who had treated the teacher flew to Kinshasa, the capital of Zaire, to seek a cure. But the doctors at Ngaliema Hospital in Kinshasa could not help her, and she also died.

The young nurse at the hospital who had been caring for the nun when the nun died was named Mayinga. She tried to protect herself from the disease by wearing gloves and a face mask, but she could not avoid contact with the nun's blood. Soon Mayinga, too, began to feel ill. But she ignored her illness and went to take care of some business at a government office, where she stood in line with hundreds of people. While waiting, she shared a bottled soft drink with a stranger. The next day, Mayinga was feeling worse. She went to Kinshasa's largest hospital, the Mama Yemo Hospital. The doctors told her she was not very sick and sent her back to Ngaliema Hospital. At the same time, rumors began to circulate throughout the city about a deadly new disease coming out of the Bumba Zone.

When people at Ngaliema Hospital realized that Mayinga had this new disease, they panicked. They alerted government officials, who became immediately alarmed. Kinshasa was a city of over two million people, with direct links by air to other cities around the world. This disease was fatal, contagious—and without a cure. It would be a disaster if it spread.

Mobutu Sese Seko, who was then president of Zaire, sent in his army to seal off the infected areas. Soldiers surrounded the Ngaliema Hospital; no one could enter or leave. All roads in the Bumba Zone were blocked. No one was allowed in or out. The World Health Organization was also alerted.

The doctors at Ngaliema Hospital drew samples of Mayinga's blood. Scientists would examine her blood to try to find and identify the mysterious germ that was killing her. The blood was placed in tightly sealed containers and carefully packed. The delicate, deadly cargo was flown to laboratories in England, Belgium, and the United States. In the United States, the blood was sent to the CDC.

The first photograph of the Zaire strain of the Ebola virus was taken in 1976 by Dr. F. A. Murphy at the CDC.

Meanwhile, an international team of epidemiologists headed to Africa. These men and women would search for everyone who had had contact with the Ebola victims. They would probe into the headwaters of the Ebola River looking for the source of the disease. The epidemiologists suspected that the disease was caused by a filovirus, a type of virus that looks like a twisting, looping string. Filoviruses appear to be far more dangerous than other types of viruses.

At the CDC, Dr. Patricia Webb and her husband, Dr. Karl M. Johnson, head of the CDC's Special Pathogens Branch, compared the blood taken from Mayinga with the inventory of blood samples stored at the CDC. Working in a tightly sealed Level 4 laboratory, the scientists identified the virus. This was a new strain, similar to an Ebola virus that had appeared in Sudan, Africa, a few months earlier—though that had not been nearly as speedy or deadly a killer. The new strain also resembled the Marburg virus, which had also originated in Africa. Dr. Johnson named it the Zaire strain of the Ebola virus.

Immediately, Dr. Johnson and a team from the CDC were dispatched to Zaire to battle the disease. Meanwhile, the international team of epidemiologists in Kinshasa was locating all persons who had had contact with Mayinga. Remarkably, none of those she had seen outside the hospital, including the boy who shared a soft drink from the same bottle, were ill. But unfortunately, Mayinga died.

In the Bumba Zone, tribal elders put in place a technique they had used over the years to combat other contagious diseases. They separated the sick people from the healthy—a form of quarantine. Villagers who became ill were confined to a hut. No well person could go near them. If the victims survived, that was fine. If they did not survive, they were left in the hut, and the hut and the bodies were burned. By doing this, the villagers were able to stop the spread of Ebola.

Two months later, the virus retreated back into the jungles as mysteriously as it had appeared. The scientists who searched for the source of Ebola did not find it. Since then, there have been a few outbreaks in sub-Saharan Africa, one as recently as 1995. But the source of this killer remains unknown.

In 1989, a similar filovirus was discovered in laboratory monkeys at Hazelton Laboratories in Reston, Virginia. Immediately, the U.S. Army Medical Research Institute of Infectious Diseases (USAMRIID) was called in to quarantine the area and

A woman waits in the emergency ward of Kikwit General Hospital in Zaire in May 1995 to find out if she has the Ebola virus.

destroy the infected monkeys. Officials tracked everyone who had had contact with the infected monkeys.

Apparently, this strain of the virus, the Reston strain, was not harmful to humans. This was very fortunate, because in such a densely populated area, the virus could have triggered a massive and deadly outbreak.

DESERT SCARE

The place where the boundaries of Colorado, Utah, Arizona, and New Mexico meet is called the Four Corners area. If you stand in the spot where you can touch four states at once, you will see a jagged red desert stretching to the horizon, a land marked by angular peaks and rough canyons. This land is the home of the Navajo Indians.

In May 1993, a healthy 24-year-old Navajo woman from Gallup, New Mexico, suddenly began to gasp for air. She had a high fever and an overwhelming headache. Her family rushed her to a nearby Indian Health Service clinic. But doctors' efforts to save her failed. She died within a few days.

Two days after her death, the woman's boyfriend suffered the same respiratory (lung) ailment while riding in the car with his family on the way to her funeral. Before they could reach medical help, he died. Within the week, two of the woman's neighbors—a young man and a young woman—also died of the same illness.

Something very strange and frightening was happening. At first, doctors suspected bubonic plague, the scourge of the Middle Ages. The plague had appeared from time to time in isolated cases among the Navajos. But no more than one or two cases had occurred at a time, and they had been treated with antibiotics. Dr. Bruce Tempest, a physician with the Indian Health Service, began calling all the clinics on the large Navajo reservation to find out if they had encountered similar cases. He learned that there were indeed other cases of this sudden, deadly respiratory attack.

Dr. Jim Cheek, an epidemiologist with the Indian Health Service, was soon in his laboratory looking under a microscope at slides of fluid samples taken from the five victims. His first hunch, too, was that this could be a reemergence of bubonic plague—but the lab reports showed no plague bacteria.

Dr. Cheek continued his detective work. He wondered if the

disease could have been caused by exposure to a toxic chemical. His computer search turned up the name of a chemical called phosgene that could have caused the victims' symptoms. Dr. Cheek traveled to the home of one young man who had died and conducted a full search of the trailer where he and his family lived. The entire family had abandoned the trailer, fearing for their lives. There was no trace of the suspected chemical, but

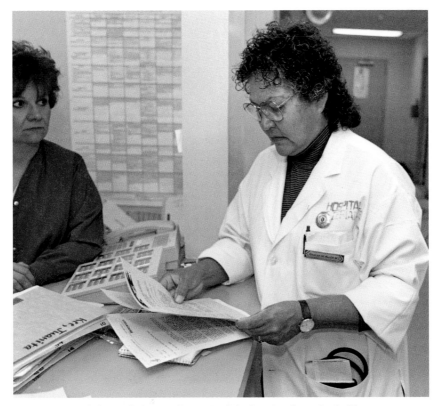

Dr. Beulah Allen of the Indian Health Service hospital. She was one of many medical experts eager to uncover the mysterious disease that appeared in 1993 among the Navajos.

the search did reveal an unusually large number of mouse droppings around the trailer, on the floor, and on the shelves.

Dr. Cheek understood what he needed to do to stop an unexplained epidemic. He would have to ask a lot of questions to find the common denominator among the victims. On the other hand, being Native American himself, he could understand the challenges he might encounter in his investigation because of Navajo beliefs about death. Although Dr. Cheek was a Cherokee, he knew that for the Navajos, it was taboo to speak of the dead or even to say the person's name for many days after the death. Dr. Cheek realized that there were many questions he could not ask.

At the same time, the Indian Health Service and the state of New Mexico had turned to the CDC for help. Dr. Jay Butler and two of his CDC associates flew to Albuquerque, New Mexico, to coordinate the investigation. Within a day, they had assem-

Dr. Jim Cheek, an epidemiologist with the Indian Health Service

bled 40 colleagues from the New Mexico Department of Health, the University of New Mexico Medical School, and the Indian Health Service. They set out to discover what was causing these deaths.

Meanwhile, another epidemiologist, Dr. Rob Breimen, and his colleagues at the CDC were reviewing the information they had. Their best guess was that the culprit was a virus. To support their theory, they had to eliminate all other possible causes they could identify. Early on, Dr. Cheek had considered the chemical phosgene, which was often used to kill prairie dogs. But after investigating, he found that no one had used this poison in the areas of the outbreak. Further study showed that while exposure to phosgene could produce most of the symptoms of this disease, it did not cause fever. The investigators ruled out phosgene as a cause. Next, they began to try to identify a virus by examining blood samples from the young men and women who had died. They carried out their work in the CDC's Level 3 and 4 laboratories.

Dr. Cheek and Dr. Butler, along with other epidemiologists, began interviewing friends and relatives of those who had died. But information was hard to get because of the taboo against talking about the dead. To make matters more difficult, television and newspaper reporters from all over the country were swarming into the area and producing alarming stories. They called the new disease "Navajo flu," which angered the citizens of the area and made them even more reluctant to talk to outsiders. The publicity caused a mini panic. People began to avoid the Four Corners area, and rumors spread that the Navajo Indians were carriers of a contagious disease.

By June 2, 1993, 12 people had died—and not all were Navajo Indians. The CDC laboratory researchers had grown cultures of viruses taken from blood samples and had begun the matching process. Soon they identified a category of viruses known as hantaviruses as the culprit. But all known hantaviruses caused kidney problems, not lung problems. All of the victims had died of respiratory problems. The investigators realized that they were facing something new. Based on what they knew about other hantaviruses, however, they suspected the source of this one to be some type of animal—most likely a rodent.

Dr. Cheek continued his work in New Mexico. Along with the Indian Health Service director and a Navajo doctor, Dr. Cheek sought help from tribal elders and other Navajos. The investigators wanted to know if there were any new tribal practices. Had anyone traveled to other places recently? Had any new foods been brought into the area? Had anyone seen unusual animals or pets in the area? Did anything happen that year that was different from other years?

After asking many questions, the team learned that the piñon nut harvest had been unusually large that year. (Piñon nuts are the edible seeds of the piñon tree, a pine tree common in the southwestern United States.) In turn, the rodent population had increased, since mice and rats thrived on piñons.

The disease detectives went out to gather samples of every type of rodent they could find. More than a hundred scientists, doctors, and animal trappers scoured the Four Corners area searching for clues and gathering a wide assortment of rodents. They drew blood samples from the rodents and shipped the samples to Atlanta for examination.

As the summer wore on, over 20,000 rodent blood samples were catalogued. Meanwhile, deaths from the new disease occurred elsewhere in the United States—a grandmother in

Texas, a woman in Nevada, a boy in Oregon. In each case, mouse droppings were discovered near the victims.

Epidemiologists came to believe that the cause of the disease was a new strain of virus carried by deer mice and spread by contact with the droppings of the infected mice. But it was not until the end of 1993 that the microbe was identified as Muerto Canyon virus, named for the canyon on the Navajo reservation where the virus first appeared. Muerto Canyon means "valley of death." The disease was stopped from spreading by getting rid of mice and mouse droppings in homes.

Chapter Six

AIDS: THE MODERN PANDEMIC

One of the worst epidemics of all time, AIDS spread around the entire world within 20 years. It is the modern pandemic. AIDS—acquired immunodeficiency syndrome—is caused by the human immunodeficiency virus, or HIV.

Isolated cases of AIDS had probably appeared in central Africa as early as the 1970s, but the HIV virus was not identified until 1984. The first clues appeared in 1981. Dr. Michael Gottlieb, an assistant professor of medicine at the University of California at Los Angeles, noticed five cases of pneumonia among young men whom he saw in his clinical practice.

There were some mystifying things about these cases. First, all the men were homosexual. Second, their pneumonia was caused by a type of parasite that is normally held in check by the body's immune system. In other words, a parasite that was not usually harmful had suddenly become lethal. Dr. Gottlieb also noted that the patients' white blood cell counts were down instead of elevated as they should have been with pneumonia. Dr. Gottlieb reported his findings to the CDC.

Meanwhile, in New York City, Dr. Alvin Friedman-Kien, a dermatologist at New York University Medical School, reported an outbreak of a rare cancer, Kaposi's sarcoma, among young gay men. He also found that their white blood cell counts were down.

Epidemiologists at the CDC believed that they were seeing the beginning of a new epidemic. Although the two diseases were different, they had something important in common: in

HIV, magnified 86,000 times, buds from a white blood cell (pink).

every case, the patient showed a marked decrease in white blood cells, particularly in one type of white blood cell. These cells, called T cells, act as "commanders" for other parts of the human immune system as it destroys invading microbes.

Normally, if a person has an infection, a blood test will show an increase in the number of white blood cells. In these cases, however, there was a decrease in the number of white blood cells. The immune system did not appear to be working normally. The patients had an immune deficiency. Scientists called the collection of diseases associated with this deficiency acquired immunodeficiency syndrome, or AIDS.

At first the diseases seemed somehow related to homosexuality. But in 1982, the same pattern appeared in people who had had blood transfusions and were not homosexual males. Dr. James Curran, who was monitoring the emerging epidemic from his office at the CDC, traveled to the National Institutes of Health in Bethesda, Maryland, to encourage the researchers there to help investigate this new medical mystery.

His presentation caught the attention of Dr. Robert Gallo, a virologist at the National Cancer Institute. The suspected culprit was a new microbe. Dr. Gallo and his staff began a search to find the microbe that was causing AIDS. Shortly after reading reports from Dr. Gallo, Dr. Luc Montagnier at the Pasteur Institute in France began pursuing the same route of research.

At that time, there were many theories about the cause of AIDS. Some people thought that several diseases were striking the patients at the same time, putting their immune systems into some form of "overload." Others offered a wide range of possible culprits, including Agent Orange, a chemical that was used in the Vietnam War; the wrath of God; an African swine fever released by the Central Intelligence Agency; and a virus

Dr. Robert Gallo led a team of researchers who identified the virus responsible for AIDS.

manufactured by the U.S. government or the Soviet Union for germ warfare. None of these theories was correct.

For the next two years, researchers working for Dr. Gallo and for Dr. Montagnier tried to find the cause. In April 1984, they found the answer. They called the virus responsible for AIDS the human immunodeficiency virus, or HIV.

With the discovery of HIV, it was possible to begin the process of tracing its origin. In Africa, AIDS was already rampant, but doctors had not recognized it as a distinct syndrome because its victims were dying of a variety of other illnesses, such as cancer and pneumonia. No one had considered that a single virus could be responsible for all these deaths.

Blood tests revealed that as much as 12 percent of the

population of the Democratic Republic of the Congo carried HIV. Other tests showed that HIV was similar to a virus found in the kidneys of some African green monkeys living in that region. Scientists theorized that the disease, after passing from monkeys to humans, had been carried to Europe by medical personnel working in Africa. It had also traveled to Haiti with Haitians who had worked in Zaire in 1970. From Haiti, it appears that the virus traveled to America with tourists visiting Haiti. Over the years, it has spread to countries all over the world, hitting Africa and Asia especially hard.

How HIV Works

The human immune system is an army of millions and millions of white blood cells working with antibodies to fight disease. It is controlled by white blood cells known as helper T cells. Helper T cells send messages to other white blood cells, directing the fight against invading microbes. One way HIV infects the body is by invading these helper T cells. The virus's DNA changes the DNA in the T cell's control centers, and the T cell begins to produce the virus. Buds of the virus grow from the cell membrane. These buds split off and develop into more viruses, which go on to enter more and more helper T cells.

As HIV takes over helper T cells, the immune system begins to shut down. Without a properly functioning immune system, a person is an easy target for other diseases. Illnesses that are not harmful to a healthy person can kill people with AIDS, because their immune systems are too weak to fight back.

When HIV enters the body, it can remain dormant for up to 10 years. Unfortunately, it is still infectious. This means that the virus can be transmitted by a person who feels fine and has

How to Prevent HIV Infection

To prevent the spread of HIV, abstain from sex and do not share intravenous (IV) drug needles. If abstinence from sex is unavoidable, do not participate in behavior that might result in contact with blood, semen, vaginal secretions, or other bodily fluids.

The following are recommended measures to prevent HIV infection:

► Do not have sex with an HIV-infected person.

► Ask about the sexual history of current and future sex partners; take HIV tests with a potential sex partner.

► Always use a condom during any type of sex (vaginal, anal, or oral). Use latex condoms and follow the directions on the package.

► Use only water-based lubricants with condoms. Do not use saliva or oil-based lubricants such as petroleum jelly.

► Avoid any sexual practice that could cut the skin and cause bleeding.

► Avoid deep, wet, or "French" kissing with an infected person. A possible cut could occur, which could result in the exchange of blood. It is safe, however, to hug, cuddle, rub, or dry kiss your partner.

► Do not share IV drug needles, syringes, or cookers.

► Do not share personal items such as toothbrushes, razors, or devices used during sex that may be contaminated with bodily fluids.

► If you are infected with HIV, have engaged in high-risk sex, or shared IV drug needles, do not donate blood, plasma, sperm, body organs, or body tissues.

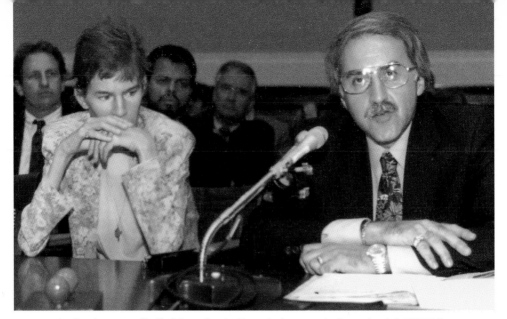

Kimberly Bergalis (left), *who believed she was infected with HIV by her dentist, traveled to Washington, D.C., in 1991 to speak to Congress in favor of mandatory HIV testing of health care workers.*

no visible signs of being sick. It is spread through bodily fluids such as blood and semen. The most common way HIV is transmitted from one person to another is through unprotected sex or by sharing hypodermic needles, a practice that is connected with drug abuse. HIV cannot survive for more than 15 minutes outside the human body. It is not transmitted on utensils, in food, by food handlers, or by touching.

It is possible to be tested to find out if you have HIV. The two most widely used tests determine if a person's blood contains antibodies to HIV.

While there is no vaccine and no cure for AIDS, some medicines can delay the onset of the disease or reduce its intensity. Many people live for many years with HIV.

In August 1996, Dr. Stephen O'Brien, a scientist at the National Cancer Institute, made a remarkable discovery. He found that for HIV to gain entry into a helper T cell, the virus must locate two different receptors on the cell. Receptors are sort of like molecular doorknobs. Both receptors must be "turned" by HIV or the virus cannot get into the cell. Some people have a defective receptor, which makes it impossible for HIV to enter their T cells. People with this "defect" are immune to AIDS. This discovery has led to exciting new research in the hunt for a way to stop the epidemic.

Scientists at Cornell University Medical College and Rockefeller University are taking a different approach. They are investigating the use of umbilical cord blood to create a safe vaccine. B cells (a kind of white blood cell) found in cord blood produce antibodies to a protein that is part of HIV. The scientists hope to use these antibodies to make a vaccine against HIV that does not include HIV itself. This is important because many scientists feel that it would be dangerous to use actual HIV virus, even in a weakened or killed form, in a vaccine.

Other approaches use various combinations, or "cocktails," of anti-HIV drugs. Such combination treatments have been successful in repressing HIV, but not in destroying it. The virus is mutating and has become resistant to some drugs.

Meanwhile, Hollis-Eden Pharmaceuticals, a biotech company in San Diego, California, is testing a drug identified as HE2000. This drug assists the patient's own immune system to battle HIV. Because HE2000 targets the immune system rather than HIV itself, HIV should not be able to resist the drug's effects.

According to the World Health Organization, over 40 million people around the world are HIV positive. Thousands more become newly infected every day because the precautions to prevent HIV infection are not understood, are not practiced, or are simply ignored. Still, the new approaches offer hope that the pandemic can be brought under control and the disease eliminated.

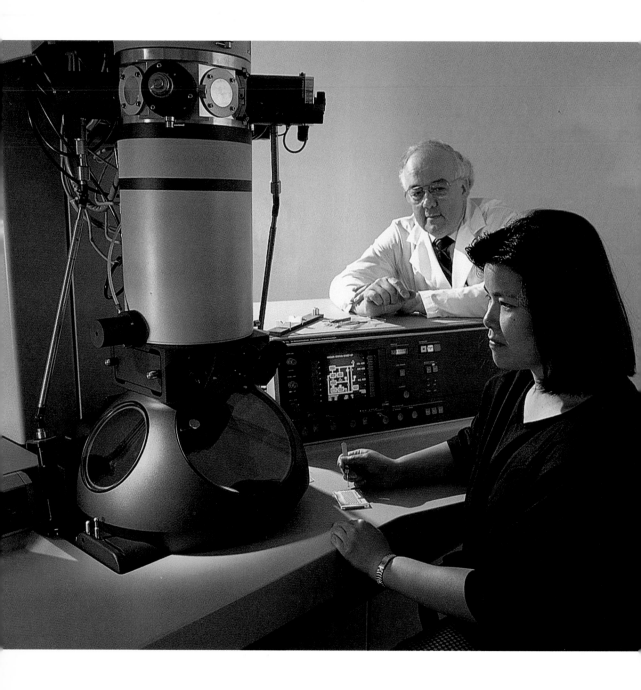

Chapter Seven

ONGOING BATTLES

As the world's growing population crowds into cities with aging water and sewage systems and we continue to pollute the water we drink and the air we breathe, the conditions are set for new plagues. Modern antibiotics and pesticides also contribute to the emergence of new microbes.

When humans chop down trees to clear land for farms and homes, microbes living in these forests lose their habitats and most find new places to live. Microbes living in animal hosts seek new hosts. If they are able to cross the species barrier to a human host, new diseases can result. Of course, throughout history microbes have moved from animals, birds, or insects to humans, bringing disease. Usually, though, the incidents were isolated, because people lived on farms and in small villages and did not travel far. In modern times, airplanes, ships, trains, and cars carry people, insects, and animals around the world faster and more frequently, sometimes carrying deadly microbes with them. In the early twenty-first century, epidemiologists will continue to rely on basic principles of epidemiology to understand and conquer new and ongoing medical mysteries.

LYME DISEASE

Most of us think of deer as graceful, gentle creatures. But these animals play a role in the spread of some infectious diseases.

A researcher prepares a slide for viewing on an electron microscope. The microscope uses a focused electron beam to form an image.

Environmental changes on the East Coast of the United States during the last two hundred years helped pave the way for diseases to jump from deer to humans.

In 1975, in the quiet, quaint town of Old Lyme, Connecticut, two children and their parents were suffering with bouts of fever, rashes, headaches, and aching joints. They were diagnosed with rheumatoid arthritis, a disease that causes inflammation, or swelling, of the joints. Usually rheumatoid arthritis affects adults, not children. The juvenile form of the disease is very rare. One of the parents, Polly Murray, learned from her neighbors that other people in the neighborhood, including several children, were also suffering the same symptoms. Murray called the Connecticut State Health Department.

This unusually high number, or cluster, of cases of juvenile rheumatoid arthritis suggested to epidemiologists that something strange was going on. Dr. Allen Steere, an arthritis specialist at the Yale University School of Medicine in New Haven, Connecticut, was called in to investigate. The incidence of juvenile rheumatoid arthritis in Old Lyme was more than one hundred times higher than the normal incidence of the disease in the general population.

Dr. Steere began a systematic search for clues by mapping the location of all reported cases and seeking some commonality among them. He assembled a team of professionals and took them to Old Lyme and the adjoining town of East Haddam. The epidemiologists learned that there had been 51 cases of rheumatoid arthritis in 1976, and 39 of the patients were children. They also learned that the disease occurred more often in the summer than in the winter. They suspected that the disease was caused by a microbe that was carried by an insect.

In 1977, Dr. Steere published a scientific paper describing

his findings. He gave the new disease the name "Lyme arthritis." So far, he did not know the cause of the disease.

Several people interviewed by epidemiologists remembered that they had been bitten by a small tick before their symptoms began. The doctors dragged cloth bags through the woods to collect ticks for analysis. The ticks were sent to a public health laboratory in Montana that specialized in tick-borne diseases. At this laboratory, Dr. Willy Burgdorfer dissected the ticks and cultured the microbes found in their bodies. He discovered the long, twisting bacterium that caused the arthritic disease. The bacterium was named after the doctor—*Borrelia burgdorferi.*

These bacteria live harmlessly in the blood of white-footed deer mice. Immature deer ticks feed on mouse blood and become infected with *Borrelia* bacteria. When a tick reaches

Borrelia burgdorferi, *the bacterium that causes Lyme disease*

adulthood, it feeds on deer. The tick may fall off a deer and end up on a human walking in the woods. Because deer ticks are extremely small—no larger than the period at the end of this sentence—people often don't even realize that they've been bitten.

When a tick bites a human and remains attached for several days to feed, it passes *Borrelia* bacteria into the human's bloodstream as it feeds off the human. At the onset of Lyme disease, a red rash may appear on the skin in a bull's-eye pattern. The person experiences flulike symptoms and later may have pain in the muscles and joints. If the disease is detected early, it is treatable with antibiotics. Untreated, it can lead to a wide range of problems, such as amnesia, changes in behavior, even fatal heart and respiratory disorders.

Deer ticks are the vectors, or carriers, of Lyme disease. They are about the size of the period at the end of this sentence.

From 1982 to 1996, more than 99,000 cases of Lyme disease were reported to the Centers for Disease Control and Prevention. In the United States, Lyme disease is most prevalent in the Northeast, upper Midwest, and along the Pacific Coast.

As the deer population and the human population both increase, the two species are more likely to come into contact with each other. Deer looking for food become bolder, often grazing in suburban backyards.

In 1999, a vaccine against Lyme disease was introduced. The vaccine must be given in three doses over a period of one year, and it is only 80 percent effective. This means that even with the vaccine, you may not be protected. Because the vaccine is still new, specialists do not know the duration of protection or whether there are long-term side effects. The vaccine is recommended only for people between the ages of 15 and 70 who are at high risk of coming into contact with deer ticks.

THE SUPERBUGS

Since bacteria are nothing more than single cells, it seems we should be able to outwit and defeat them. But that is not always the case. As single cells, bacteria can mutate and change their structure to adjust to new circumstances faster than humans can, with our complex organs and our bodies made of millions and millions of cells.

According to the theory of natural selection, organisms that can adapt to meet the challenges of a changing environment are best able to survive and reproduce, ensuring that their offspring will continue to exist. This is also called "survival of the fittest." Erasmus Darwin, a physician and naturalist, first proposed these revolutionary ideas about the evolution of plants, animals, and humans in 1790. His grandson, Charles Darwin, set out to test the theory. After finishing his studies in medicine and theology in 1831, Charles Darwin signed up to serve as a naturalist on a British scientific expedition aboard the HMS *Beagle,* a warship converted to serve as his laboratory. During the five years of the journey, Darwin gathered evidence to support his own developing ideas about natural selection. He published his findings in a book called *The Origin of Species.*

Like other creatures, microbes follow the laws of evolution. The fittest survive by making changes to adapt to new conditions. The hosts upon which microbes depend also change. The hosts' immune systems adapt and find ways to destroy the microbial invaders. These changes do not happen suddenly, however. In 1994, science writer Laurie Garrett described the process of mutation in her book, *The Coming Plague: Newly Emerging Diseases in a World Out of Balance:* "Roughly one out of every 10 million *E. coli* [bacteria] in a petri dish might randomly mutate to be resistant to, say, penicillin. Then, if the drug were poured into the petri dish, 9,999,999 bacteria would die, but that one resistant *E. coli* would survive, and divide and multiply, passing the genes for resistance on to its progeny."

The staphylococcus family of bacteria have shown a remarkable ability to become resistant to antibiotics. While staph bacteria live harmlessly on the skin of most people, the bacteria can cause a wide range of problems. These problems include boils, pneumonia, urinary tract infection, toxic shock syndrome, and arthritis. Infections from this family of bacteria are called staph infections.

In 1952, most staph infections were easily treated by the antibiotic penicillin. Forty years later, penicillin could cure only

Some strains of staphylococcus bacteria, shown here magnified 3,145 times, have become resistant to certain antibiotics. This has become a major concern among health professionals.

10 percent of staph infections in developed nations. This is because strains of staphylococcus bacteria developed resistance to penicillin—they mutated and avoided being killed by the drug. Doctors began using other antibiotics, but staph bacteria have slowly become resistant to each new antibiotic. Epidemiologists fear that a new strain of staph will emerge that will be resistant to all available antibiotics. Several other bacterial diseases are also developing antibiotic resistance.

Several factors have contributed to the development of antibiotic resistance in bacteria. First, antibiotics have been widely used as a general cure-all, sometimes even when they're unnecessary, such as in the treatment of a viral infection. (Antibiotics are effective against bacteria, but not viruses.) This widespread use of antibiotics has allowed bacteria to "hurry" the process of natural selection. And antibiotics are not always taken properly. Say, for example, a doctor prescribes penicillin to a patient with a strep throat infection. The patient takes the medicine for a few days, feels better, then stops taking it before using the prescribed amount. The problem is that all the bacteria may not have been killed. Those remaining are the "fittest." They form the beginning of a drug-resistant strain.

Second, in poorer countries, antibiotics are used for a variety of purposes—often unrelated to a drug's intended use—and without proper control. Bacteria mutate and develop resistance to the antibiotics. These "superbugs" move to different parts of the world as people travel.

Third, modern hospitals provide bacteria with an ideal breeding ground. More antibiotics are used in hospitals than anywhere else. Many people who come to the hospital are already sick, with weakened immune systems, so they are more susceptible to germs. If bacteria that are resistant to one antibiotic come in contact with bacteria that are resistant to another antibiotic, some of the bacteria may become resistant to both drugs.

In hospitals, staphylococcus bacteria are common. They can pass from person to person by contact or by touching the same utensils. In 1992, nearly one million people who underwent surgery in the United States suffered a postsurgical infection, even though hospitals uphold stringent standards for cleanliness in the operating room. An infection that develops in a hospital or other health care facility is called a nosocomial infection. Many of these infections are staph infections.

The Mobility of Genes

Each bacterium contains its own strands of DNA. The DNA instructions for building more, identical microbes are encoded in chromosomes—long strings of molecular beads containing thousands of genes. Genes control the expression and transmission of specific traits of an organism. As bacteria multiply and reproduce, genes from one bacterium are passed to the next.

In the 1940s and 1950s, geneticist Barbara McClintock *(right)* did experiments with corn plants at the Cold Spring Harbor Laboratory on Long Island, New York, to learn more about how genes work. She found that some genes were mobile—they could move within strands of DNA. When a gene changed from one place on its chromosome to another, the result was a radical change in the appearance of the corn.

Other scientists built on McClintock's work and discovered that the principle of genetic mobility also applied to other organisms, including bacteria. The mobility of genes gives bacteria another tool for developing resistance to antibiotics.

Soon after antibiotics were developed to treat human bacterial diseases, veterinarians and livestock producers began to use these same medicines to treat animals. Not only were antibiotics used to treat sick animals, but they were also given to cows, chickens, pigs, and sheep on a regular basis to keep them healthier. The health of farm animals did improve. At the same time, new strains of bacteria developed that were resistant to antibiotics.

In February 1993, Dr. Michael Osterholm, the Minnesota state epidemiologist, noticed an increase in the number of food poisoning cases in Minnesota. He traced the problem to a bacterium called *Salmonella newport*. Salmonella bacteria cause diarrhea and vomiting in humans. These flulike symptoms are usually referred to as "food poisoning." Dr. Osterholm noticed two strange things about these cases. The *newport* form of salmonella was native to the southern states near the Gulf of Mexico, far from Minnesota. He also noted that the people who fell ill with this form of salmonella poisoning were sicker than would normally be expected, and the bacteria seemed resistant to four different antibiotics.

Dr. Osterholm began an epidemiological investigation. He sent notices to other health departments around the country. He learned that there had been similar outbreaks in North and South Dakota. Each of the victims had eaten a hamburger before falling ill. Further investigation turned up 40,000 pounds of contaminated beef. The Minnesota Department of Health traced the beef to a herd of cattle that had been given antibiotics. Antibiotic-resistant salmonella bacteria had developed in these cattle, and the bacteria had passed to people who had eaten meat from the cattle.

A similar epidemic occurred with another bacterium that

causes food poisoning, *Escherichia coli (E. coli).* In Washington State, five hundred people became sick in 1993 from eating hamburgers at a particular restaurant chain. The meat had come from a herd of cattle that had been fed food laced with antibiotics.

MAD COW DISEASE

Humans face a wide range of microbes, including viruses, bacteria, and parasites. Recently, what may be a new disease-causing agent was discovered—the prion, an infectious particle of protein. Not all scientists agree that prions exist. The theory of prions stems from the study of several diseases, including one found among a tribe on a remote jungle island.

The island nation of Papua New Guinea lies in the Pacific Ocean, north of Australia, and stretches for 1,500 miles east to west. High in the mountains, protected by heavy rain forests, Melanesian farmers live in much the same way as their Stone Age ancestors did, without electricity or running water.

One of the Melanesian tribes is the Fore (pronounced FOR-ay). Fore women traditionally had the task of preparing bodies for burial. They removed and handled the brains, and sometimes they ate pieces of the brains, giving some to their children. This practice, they believed, would give them strength and wisdom.

Some Fore people developed a terrible illness. First they began to stagger when walking. Then they could not walk at all. Victims had trouble swallowing, and they died shivering and shaking. The Fore called this syndrome *kuru,* the trembling sickness. They believed that kuru was caused by evil spirits.

In 1957, Dr. D. Carleton Gajdusek, a young American pediatrician and virologist, heard about this mysterious trembling sickness. Based on the symptoms, he suspected that it might be a new disease, a new form of brain infection. Dr. Gajdusek wanted to investigate. He went into the jungle highlands of Papua New Guinea and hiked from village to village, asking questions and collecting blood and tissue samples.

Dr. Gajdusek didn't know whether the disease was genetic or if it was caused by an infectious microbe or some other agent. He wanted to autopsy the brains of people who had died of kuru to see if he could find out what caused the disease. He traded axes and tobacco for brains of dead Fore members. He saw no sign of a viral or bacterial infection in the brain tissue. But he did notice microscopic, tangled knots of protein known as amyloid plaques. These plaques are more commonly seen in people with Alzheimer's disease, a disease of aging marked by mental deterioration. The symptoms and results of kuru were most similar to those of a rare brain disease called Creutzfeldt-Jakob disease (CJD). In both kuru and CJD, the brain becomes "spongy," or full of holes, causing mental and physical deterioration in the victim.

Dr. Gajdusek believed there had to be some virus that was transmitting kuru, but he could not find an infective agent. He was able to reproduce the disease in laboratory monkeys by inoculating them with kuru-infected tissue. This suggested that the Fore people could have been infected through cuts in their hands when they touched the brains of kuru victims, or they became infected by eating the brains.

By the 1960s, the government of Papua New Guinea began to enforce a ban on cannibalism among the Fore. As the Fore people abandoned the custom of eating brains, the new generation of children was mostly free of any sign of kuru.

In 1976, Dr. Gajdusek was awarded the Nobel Prize in medicine for his research on kuru. Two years later, Dr. Stanley

Dr. D. Carleton Gajdusek (left) *accepts the 1976 Nobel Prize in medicine from King Carl Gustaf of Sweden.*

Prusiner, a biochemist and neurologist, traveled to Papua New Guinea to help Dr. Gajdusek look for the mysterious virus. Dr. Prusiner hoped to discover the cause of Creutzfeldt-Jakob disease, which he associated with a disease called scrapie, which caused brain damage in sheep.

By 1982, Dr. Prusiner was ready to present a scientific paper on his research. He declared that the cause of scrapie was an infectious protein, which he named a prion. This was, he said, an infectious protein particle containing no nucleic acid. In 1997, Dr. Prusiner was awarded a Nobel Prize for his research.

No one has ever seen a prion, even with an electron microscope. Some scientists are skeptical of the concept. Some people think these "spongy brain" diseases may be caused by a primitive kind of virus called a virino.

In 1986, as research into the cause of scrapie and kuru continued, an epidemic struck cattle in Britain. Cows with this

On May 14, 1996, the World Health Organization held a meeting of experts to discuss Creutzfeldt-Jakob disease and mad cow disease.

fatal disease changed personality. They became aggressive, nervous, and hard to handle. They lost their coordination and began to stumble. Whole herds were affected. Newspaper headlines called the syndrome "mad cow disease." The official name of the disease is bovine spongiform encephalopathy (BSE).

Epidemiologists were called in. What did two hundred cows from different parts of Britain have in common? The only common factor was their feed. The cows were given a high protein mixture that included rendered sheep—slaughtered sheep that had been ground up and processed. This food included the remains of sheep that had died of scrapie.

In 1995, Dr. James Ironside, a pathologist with the British National CJD Surveillance Unit in Edinburgh, Scotland, found amyloid plaques and spongelike holes in the brain tissue of a teenage boy who had died of Creutzfeldt-Jakob disease. Spongy holes were also the major feature of kuru and scrapie. Dr. Ironside alerted the director of the surveillance unit, Dr. Robert Will, who turned up more cases of CJD. By the end of 1996, 10 cases had appeared. At first, the patients acted "nutty," then slowly, over months, they began to stagger, tremble, and ultimately die. Epidemiologists feared that an infectious agent had spread from cattle to humans when people ate beef from BSE-infected cattle.

The British cabinet convened emergency sessions of Parliament, the highest legislative body of Great Britain. On March 19, 1996, Stephen Dorrell, the Secretary of State for Health, stood in the House of Commons and announced to Parliament, and the world, that BSE might have spread from cattle to humans in the form of Creutzfeldt-Jakob disease. In the United States, the Food and Drug Administration issued regulations to protect Americans from the possible spread of mad cow disease. The regulations forbade the use of slaughtered and processed animals in food for cows, sheep, or goats. In Britain, the number of BSE-infected cattle declined sharply because of tough rules regulating farms. Scientists still do not know whether the causative agent of these spongiform diseases is a prion, a slow-acting virus, a virino, or some new form of microbe.

Chapter Eight

BIOTERRORISM

Bioterrorism is the use of deadly germs to kill or terrorize an enemy. The word is a relatively recent addition to the English language, but the concept has been around for thousands of years.

Without having any concept of "germs," warriors in many ancient civilizations engaged in acts of bioterrorism. Both the Greeks and the Romans threw carcasses of diseased animals into their enemies' water supplies in order to spread disease and death. The Muslim warriors who catapulted dead plague victims over the walls of Kaffa in the 1300s were also bioterrorists.

The first documented biological warfare in American history took place during the French and Indian War. Lord Jeffrey Amherst, commander of the British forces in North America, suggested the use of smallpox as a weapon against the Indians. When the disease broke out at Fort Pitt (now Pittsburgh) in 1763, smallpox-infected blankets were given to warriors from a local Indian tribe. The gift was followed by an epidemic among the tribes along the Ohio River, killing half of their population.

When Japan invaded Manchuria in the early 1930s, it began a biological warfare research program using Chinese prisoners as guinea pigs. From 1932 until the end of World War II in 1945, Japan operated an infamous research facility code-named Unit 731. During the 13 years that this program was in operation, over 10,000 prisoners died of experimental infections or direct

Hazardous materials unit workers take turns hosing one another down. The unit is inspecting government buildings in Washington, D.C., for anthrax contamination during the October 2001 anthrax scare.

execution. Unit 731 also conducted large-scale experiments. In one, plague-infected fleas were released from airplanes flying over Chinese cities to cause epidemics of bubonic plague.

Also during World War II, an American biological warfare research program was begun at Fort Detrick (then Camp Detrick) in Maryland. The work continued after the war ended.

In 1972, more than one hundred nations, including the United States, Iraq, and the Soviet Union, signed the Biological Weapons Convention. This treaty prohibited the development and use of biological weapons. Despite the treaty, the Soviet Union and Iraq each continued to develop biological weapons. The Russian program, Biopreparat, had the capacity to produce large quantities of smallpox, plague, and anthrax microbes.

Although nations such as Russia, Iraq, Iran, Syria, and North Korea have continued to develop biological weapons, none has actually used these weapons in an attack. Rather, small groups and individuals have become the bioterrorists. For example, in 1984, followers of Indian guru Bhagwan Shree Rajneesh intentionally contaminated salad bars in 10 restaurants in The Dalles, Oregon, with salmonella bacteria, causing 751 people to fall ill. The purpose of the assault was to test the cult's biowarfare techniques. The outbreak brought large numbers of epidemiologists to The Dalles, making further attacks impossible.

POTENTIAL WEAPONS FOR BIOWARFARE

The CDC has identified 18 classes of diseases that are the most likely to be used in biowarfare. Only a handful of these would be effective on a large scale. In order for a microbe to be used as an agent of mass destruction it must cause illness or death, a delivery system must be available, and the public must not be immune to it. Anthrax, smallpox, tularemia, and botulism, and, to a lesser extent, bubonic plague and viral hemorrhagic fevers, are the microbes most likely to be used by bioterrorists.

Anthrax is the bioterrorist weapon of choice. A small amount can easily be used to cause widespread danger and disruption. If the symptoms are quickly recognized and diagnosed by health authorities, however, such an outbreak can be contained.

The first anthrax attack on America came as a surprise. On October 5, 2001, Robert Stevens, a photo editor for a tabloid publishing company in Boca Raton, Florida, died of inhalation anthrax. A mailroom clerk in the same publishing house was also diagnosed with anthrax, but he recovered.

Following the diagnosis of inhalation anthrax in Florida, the CDC was on high alert. At first, natural causes were assumed. But then an NBC employee in New York City was diagnosed with cutaneous anthrax after she opened a letter containing a powdery substance. It became clear that bioterrorists were responsible. Within days the largest force of disease detectives ever assembled began investigating the anthrax attacks.

Soon two more anthrax-laced letters appeared, one addressed to Senate Majority Leader Thomas Daschle and the other to Senator Patrick Leahy. These letters had been processed at the Brentwood mail distribution center in Washington, D.C. Anthrax spores leaked from the letters during handling, contaminating other mail and exposing postal workers to the attack.

Health officials closed several buildings for fumigation. Tens of thousands of letters were shipped to Ohio for irradiation to kill anthrax spores. Thousands of postal workers and government office workers were examined for the presence of anthrax and given a 60-day regimen of the antibiotic ciprofloxacin. At-risk workers were also offered an as-yet-unlicensed anthrax vaccine. By the time the emergency was over, a few spore-filled letters had indirectly affected thousands of people, disrupted government and commerce, and directly infected at least 11 people with inhalation anthrax, killing 5.

The use of smallpox virus as an agent of terrorism has become an ominous possibility. Routine smallpox vaccinations were discontinued in the United States in 1972 and worldwide in 1984. Because immunity due to vaccination decreases over time, even those who were vaccinated may have lost their immunity. There is a limited supply of smallpox vaccine, and no effective cure. After the 2001 anthrax attacks, the U.S. government began a massive program to produce millions of vials of vaccine to be ready for a terrorist attack involving smallpox.

If smallpox microbes were sprayed into the air and infected only 50 to 100 people, the disease could spread person-to-person to thousands of people within weeks. Quick diagnosis, immediate identification of the source of the virus, complete quarantine of all contacted persons, and a well-organized vaccination plan would be necessary to contain the outbreak.

Botulism is caused by a bacterium, *Clostridium botulinum,* which produces botulinum toxin, one of nature's deadliest poisons. Botulism is principally associated with improperly prepared or handled foods. Any airborne delivery of botulism bacteria would signal a bioterrorist attack. Iran, Iraq, North Korea, and Syria have developed or are believed to have developed botulinum toxin as a weapon, as well as methods to deploy it.

Tularemia, or rabbit fever, is a highly infectious disease caused by the bacterium *Francisella tularensis.* In nature, tularemia is carried by rodents, rabbits, and hares that have been infected by ticks, flies, or mosquitoes. The disease is transmitted to humans who are bitten by infected ticks or insects, handle infected animals, or drink contaminated water. It is not transmitted from person to person. Because of the low natural incidence of tularemia, any sudden outbreak would be suspected of being caused by bioterrorists.

Bubonic plague and viral hemorrhagic fevers (VHFs) are also possible candidates for bioterrorist use. VHFs are caused by several different families of viruses. Some of these diseases are relatively mild, but others, such as Ebola hemorrhagic fever, are life threatening. VHFs are naturally found in animal hosts but can be transmitted to humans. Some VHFs can also be transmitted from human to human. Plague and VHFs are harder to incorporate into attack mechanisms and harder to control once released than anthrax, smallpox, tularemia, or botulism, so they are not as attractive to bioterrorists. The threat of these diseases is not, however, overlooked by the organizations focused upon protecting America from the military use of deadly microbes.

BIOTERRORISM AND EPIDEMIOLOGISTS

Bioterrorism presents the greatest challenge to epidemiologists. In the wake of the 2001 terrorist attacks, the CDC urged heightened surveillance. Health care professionals must immediately report cases of any of the potential bioterror diseases to the epidemiological centers in their state or directly to the CDC.

Likely the first warning of any clandestine bioterrorist attack would be a sudden, unusual cluster of cases of one of the suspect diseases. Because there is a delay between exposure to a terrorist's release of microbes and the actual outbreak of a disease in a population, time is critical. Unusual patterns of disease must be considered with great suspicion and met with a rapid response. This is the role of America's disease detectives.

EPIDEMIOLOGY AND THE FUTURE

Infectious disease epidemiologists are our sentinels, guarding against some of humanity's most dangerous enemies—microbes. These minuscule organisms have caused more harm to more people throughout history than all wars combined.

One hundred years ago, deaths from infectious diseases were still commonplace all over the world. By the end of World War II, however, scientists had an array of weapons for battling microbes—antibiotics, vaccinations, and improved sanitation. Many diseases, such as whooping cough and diphtheria, had practically disappeared. The great plagues that had ravaged whole populations—smallpox, typhus, typhoid fever, measles— had been virtually conquered. Following the American lead, other countries began to use DDT and other pesticides to control mosquitoes and prevent the spread of malaria. By the 1960s, most Americans believed that modern science had brought the threat of epidemics to an end.

While we were "conquering" disease, bacteria and viruses were quietly evolving and adapting. Microbes are not smarter than we are, but they have been around much longer. They are also less complex, so they can mutate and evolve faster than we can. Bacteria that have survived death by antibiotics become superbugs, resistant to our most powerful drugs. Viruses change their shape to survive. Some of our old enemies are returning with a vengeance.

Because of environmental changes and human mobility, new

epidemics such as AIDS have spread around the globe. Tuber-culosis is on the rise again, and new outbreaks of ancient epidemics—cholera, malaria, yellow fever, diphtheria, and influenza—are making headlines again. Deadly viruses like Ebola have leaped out of their jungle habitats.

Still, the remarkable skills of disease detectives help to pre-vent widespread medical disasters. Their understanding of how diseases spread helps keep us safe from our invisible enemies. While the danger of microbial invasion is real, epidemiologists are watching for signs of an epidemic and are ready to take action to stop the threat.

GLOSSARY

AIDS (acquired immunodeficiency syndrome)—a collection of diseases caused by the human immunodeficiency virus (HIV), which attacks and destroys the helper T cells of the immune system

anthrax—a disease caused by the bacterium *Bacillus anthracis*. It primarily affects plant-eating animals such as cattle and sheep, but it can be transmitted to humans.

antibiotics—medicines used to treat bacterial infections

antibodies—molecular proteins that attack and destroy specific microbes that invade the human body

bacteria—single-celled microorganisms that live in soil, water, plants, animals, and humans and can cause disease

bioterrorism—the use of deadly germs to kill or terrorize an enemy

botulism—a disease usually associated with improperly prepared or handled foods; caused by the *Clostridium botulinum* bacterium

bovine spongiform encephalopathy (BSE)—a disease that affects cattle, causing their brains to have a spongelike appearance and resulting in loss of coordination due to brain damage; also called "mad cow disease"

bubonic plague—a disease caused by the *Yersinia pestis* bacterium, spread by fleas from rats, which caused widespread death during the Middle Ages; also called Black Death

cholera—a disease caused by *Vibrio cholerae* bacteria, which live in contaminated water. Cholera causes severe diarrhea, vomiting, and fever and is often fatal.

Creutzfeldt-Jakob disease (CJD)—a fatal, progressive degeneration of the brain characterized by lack of coordination, seizures, confusion, and spongelike (spongiform) formations in the brain

culture—nutrients used to grow microorganisms in a laboratory

diphtheria—an infectious, often fatal disease that causes swelling of the throat and tonsils, difficulty breathing, and high fever; caused by the *Corynebacterium diphtheriae* bacterium

DNA (deoxyribonucleic acid)—a molecule in the nuclei of cells that contains instructions determining the characteristics of organisms

Ebola—a family of viruses that cause deadly hemorrhagic diseases (diseases characterized by internal bleeding)

epidemic—an unusually high incidence of a disease or illness among a community of people

epidemiology—the study of disease and health in populations

filovirus—a type of virus that looks like a twisting, looping string

fungi—spore-producing organisms that lack chlorophyll, usually classified as plants. There are over one hundred thousand species of fungi, including yeasts, molds, smuts, and mushrooms.

hantaviruses—a family of viruses that cause hemorrhagic fever diseases, usually characterized by fever, weakness, fatigue, internal bleeding, and kidney failure. These viruses are carried by rodents.

HIV (human immunodeficiency virus)—the virus that causes acquired immunodeficiency syndrome (AIDS)

immune system—the units of the body, especially white blood cells, that work together to fight disease

immunity—resistance to a disease

infection—the reproduction of microbes in the body

infectious diseases—illnesses that can be spread or transmitted

influenza—a viral disease resulting in high fever, muscle aches, chest congestion, and intestinal irritation; usually called "the flu"

kuru—a disease found among members of the Fore tribe in Papua New Guinea. Symptoms begin with shivering, followed by loss of the ability to walk and swallow, and finally death.

Legionnaires' disease—a lung infection caused by the *Legionnella pneumophila* bacterium

Lyme disease—a disease caused by the *Borrelia burgdorferi* bacterium and spread by the bite of the deer tick

malaria—a disease that occurs in tropical and subtropical regions and is spread through the bite of female *Anopheles* mosquitoes

microbes—the general term applied to organisms, such as bacteria and viruses, that are too small to be seen by the naked eye

Muerto Canyon virus—a hantavirus that spreads through contact with dust from the feces of deer mice

mutate—to undergo a change in molecular structure that is continued in succeeding generations of the organism

pandemic—an epidemic that spreads to an entire country or continent, or to the whole world

parasites—organisms that feed on or live in other organisms

prion—thought to be an infectious protein with no nucleic acid

protozoa—single-celled microscopic organisms; some are parasites

quarantine—isolation of a person or group of people suspected of being infected with a disease to prevent the spread of that disease

quinine—a medicine produced from the bark of cinchona trees; used to treat malaria

rickettsia—a group of bacteria that act like viruses in the way they attack human cells. They cause a number of diseases, such as Rocky Mountain spotted fever and typhus.

RNA (ribonucleic acid)—molecules in the nucleus of a cell that control the cell's chemical activities

salmonella—a group of bacteria that cause food poisoning, intestinal inflammation, typhoid fever, or septicemia (blood poisoning)

smallpox—an often fatal infectious disease marked by chills, high fever, and pus-filled blisters; eradicated worldwide since 1980

statistical association—a finding by an epidemiologic study of an increased number of cases of a disease or condition within a selected population who share one or more characteristics

tularemia—a highly infectious disease caused by the *Francisella tularensis* bacterium; also called rabbit fever

vaccine—a preparation of killed or weakened microorganisms that provides protection from a particular disease

viral hemorrhagic fevers (VHFs)—a group of viral diseases characterized by sudden onset, fever, aching, and internal bleeding

virologists—scientists who study viruses

virus—the smallest and simplest kind of life-form; a protein shell containing a core of nucleic acid

FOR FURTHER READING

BOOKS AND MAGAZINE ARTICLES

Biel, Timothy L. *The Black Death.* San Diego: Lucent Books, 1989.

Friedlander Jr., Mark P., and Terry M. Phillips. *The Immune System: Your Body's Disease-Fighting Army.* Minneapolis: Lerner Publications, 1998.

Giblin, James Cross. *When Plague Strikes: The Black Death, Smallpox, AIDS.* New York: HarperCollins, 1995.

Jaret, Peter. "The Disease Detectives." *National Geographic,* January 1991, 114.

Karlen, Arno. *Man and Microbes.* New York: Putnam, 1995.

Preston, Richard. *The Hot Zone.* New York: Random House, 1994.

Rhodes, Richard. *Deadly Beasts: Tracking the Secrets of a Terrifying New Plague.* New York: Simon and Schuster, 1997.

Silverstein, Alvin, Virginia Silverstein, and Robert Silverstein. *Lyme Disease: the Great Imitator.* Lebanon, NJ: Avstar, 1990.

Storad, Conrad J. *Inside AIDS: HIV Attacks the Immune System.* Minneapolis: Lerner Publications, 1998.

Yancey, Diane. *The Hunt for Hidden Killers: Ten Cases of Medical Mystery.* Brookfield, CT: Millbrook, 1994.

WEBSITES

A Beef with Beef <http://whyfiles.org/012mad_cow/index.html>

AIDS & Young People <http://www.avert.org/young.htm>

Centers for Disease Control and Prevention <http://www.cdc.gov>

Epidemic! On the Trail of Killer Diseases <http://www.discovery.com/exp /epidemic/epidemic.html>

INDEX

ABOUT THE AUTHOR

Mark P. Friedlander Jr. has been a trial attorney in Washington, D.C., and northern Virginia for over 40 years. As a lawyer, he played a major role in the litigation that followed the swine flu epidemic of 1976 that never occurred and the massive vaccination program that wasn't needed. He is the author of several books, including *The Immune System* and *When Objects Talk,* in Lerner's Discovery! series.

PHOTO ACKNOWLEDGMENTS

© Centers for Disease Control and Prevention, Atlanta, pp. 1, 23, 24, 47, 58, 95, 107; **Peter Arnold, Inc.:** (© Jim Olive) p. 2, (© Nicole Duplaix) p. 40 (right), (© Alfred Pasieka) p. 63 (left), (© Volker Steger) p. 101, (© David Scharf) p. 105, (© CSHL Archives) p. 107 (inset); © Corbis/Bettmann-Gendreau, p. 8; **Photo Researchers, Inc.:** (© TEK Image/Science Photo Library) p. 12, (© Dr. Gopal Murti/Science Photo Library) p. 26, (© Kul Bhatia) p. 32 (right), (© Science Photo Library) pp. 33, 56, (© Jean-Loup Charmet/Science Photo Library) p. 34, (© Alfred Pasieka/Science Photo Library) pp. 40 (right), 69, (© National Library of Medicine/Science Photo Library) p. 45, (© London School of Hygiene/Science Photo Library) p. 55 (left), (© Sinclair Stammers/Science Photo Library) p. 55 (right), (© NIBSC/Science Photo Library) pp. 63 (right), 90, (© Mark Newman) p. 72, (© Dr. Linda Stannard, UCT/Science Photo Library) p. 74, (© Scott Camazine) pp. 81, 102 (right), (© N.C.I./Science Source) p. 93, (© James Prince) p. 98, (© Hank Morgan) p. 102 (left); © New York Public Library, p. 17; illustration by Laura Westlund, p. 29; © Archive Photos, p. 32 (left); © Scala/Art Resource, NY, p. 37; © Corbis/Bettmann, p. 44; © UPI/Corbis-Bettmann, pp. 48, 52, 96, © Independent Picture Service, p. 59; © Corbis/Bettmann-UPI, p. 66, © AP/Wide World Photos, pp. 77, 85, 111, 112, 114; © REUTERS/Jean-Marc Bouju/Archive Photos, p. 83, Courtesy of Dr. Jim Cheek, p. 86.

Front cover: © Photo Researchers, Inc./Dr. Linda Stannard, UCT/Science Photo Library.